THE LAST VALLEY

A story of God's grace in terminal illness

GRAHAM HEAPS

EP Books (Evangelical Press), Registered Office: 140 Coniscliffe Road,
Darlington, Co Durham DL3 7RT

admin@epbooks.org

www.epbooks.org

EP Books are distributed in the USA by:

JPL Books, 3883 Linden Ave. S.E., Wyoming, MI 49548

order@jplbooks.com

www.jplbooks.com

British Library Cataloguing in Publication Data available

Print ISBN978-1-78397-296-8

When through the deep waters I cause you to go,
the rivers of grief shall not you overflow;
For I will be with you, your troubles to bless,
And sanctify to you your deepest distress.

How firm a foundation, you saints of the Lord 'K' in Rippon's
Selection, 1787 (this version v4 in Christian Hymns, ©
Evangelical Movement of Wales and Christian Hymns
Committee 2004)

Contents

This book is dedicated to:

Angela Donnelly, Chris Howey and Christine Tyler.
You are ladies whose company my Sue treasured, perhaps
above all her many friends.
And you proved so wonderfully faithful and supportive in
her greatest time of need.
May God bless you!

Foreword

I've read this book, every word. I couldn't put it down. I have known its author for forty years, and also his wife for those same long and happy decades. There are few people I have admired as much. A year after Sue died my own dear wife Iola also died. I have walked the same valley as Graham, but what tenderness, kindness, patience and self-disparagement he has shown, and what submission to the good and acceptable and perfect will of God. I would have given all the world to write this book as Graham expresses himself here.

I will read the book again. It will be a delight to do so. It will strengthen my hope, and deepen my trust in God, learning how Graham Heaps was given strength and wisdom when confronted with the greatest test of his life, walking with the one he adored right up to that river, across which there is no bridge, and see her slip away to glory unable yet to go with her any further.

There are observations on every page that humbled me, but also strengthened me in trusting a living personal Father in heaven who can never wrong me, nor mine, in anything he does. I am so thankful for the courage and honesty of Graham as he shares this pilgrimage with us. God was teaching him, his dear family and a huge circle of admirers the most important lessons of life: that those who do so much for their dying friends and family are precisely the people whose hopes are firmly set on the world to come.

The Christian hope fills these pages, and so it is not a morbid book, though it can bring tears to your eyes as you read it. It is a book of hope, that what we witness here we must all face for ourselves and also for those we love most, but the Lord Jesus has risen from the dead. He is ultimate reality, not death. And he has won a delightful future for all those whose trust is in him.

There will be no more sickness; no more death; no more sobs; no more partings. We will love and play and leap for joy without the interference of sin. All that causes us pain, shame and regret will be banished for ever. We will enjoy our ego-free hearts, with no self-pity and grumbling excuses. We will never have confused minds again, and will have disease-free bodies. We will see God in Jesus Christ and be loved by the Father and the Son and the Holy Spirit, and know that we are loved. We will enjoy what is most enjoyable with unbounded energy and passion for ever and ever. We will rest and work: we will worship and create: we will renew old friendship with the purest delight. We will want that life to go on for ever, and it will. That is the hope the mere believer in Jesus Christ has in death and eternity. That hope was rekindled as I read these pages.

I will use this book. There are people I have in mind now who will receive copies of this book. I am convinced they will receive much help from reading it. It will do pastoral and therapeutic good while it is in print, and I can never see it being out of print. There seems to me a blessing from God attending what is recorded in these pages. Please taste it. Read the first page or two and get the feel of two ordinary people who meet, fall in love and live a richly fulfilling and modest life, serving, caring and enjoying all that God brings to them, to the very end.

Geoff Thomas (Amyand Park Chapel, Twickenham, London)

Introduction

It is vital, at the outset of your journey into this slim volume to give you, my reader, an idea of the story that lies in your hands. Here you will find an honest, gritty, and at times somewhat harrowing, eyewitness account of how my precious wife of more than forty years struggled with a malignant, rapidly spreading, and seemingly all-conquering brain tumour. You will learn how she came to terms with her condition, and how she coped with its increasingly debilitating effects up until the day it took her life, around a year after her alarming symptoms first appeared.

The account also shows the effect of the shock diagnosis, brutal operation, unexpectedly long hospitalisation, brief recovery and subsequent decline on her large family and many friends. What I have written is a deeply personal account of tough days. It is honestly recorded, but reflects the way I saw things; how each twist in the road affected me. As such it is full of vivid memories of my own experience of horror and hope, panic and peace, fear and faith, consternation and comfort.

To be completely candid, here you will find a loving husband's view of his wife's struggles with a vile affliction, and doubtless that love colours every line of the record that I have written, as it did every moment of the experience itself. Indeed the account is, unashamedly, a love story: the record of how a relationship, already strong and satisfying, was not only sustained but seemed to flower yet more beautifully, in the bitter winds and sleety showers of a horrific terminal illness.

Supremely, however, this is a story of discovery. It traces how two very ordinary and, indeed, timid and flawed Christians learned at first-hand the truth of God's striking promise to presence himself with his sheep as they walk in the intimidating 'valley of the shadow of death.' Together we were surprised by grace in the furnace of approaching death and its dreaded separation. And if you patiently come with me all the way to the final pages of my little book, you will learn how a grieving widower was wonderfully upheld, generally preserved from corrosive bitterness, and even brought into new joys, by the same gracious hand of the Good Shepherd.

I have made public our story in the hope that it may be of some help to those who have to walk in similar tough tracks, or who greatly fear that this may be their lot one day. Its main purpose is to show anyone who wants to know where the best help, and only true comfort, can be found, and to reassure those who love and follow the Saviour that he will not fail them in life's darkest moments. If the account proves to be of any help at all, I shall be more than satisfied.

Finally, it needs to be added that if the account is helpful, or even readable and coherent, much of the credit goes to my dear friend and initial editorial advisor, Gwyn Davies of Aberystwyth. Gwyn, who knew Sue all her adult life, went through the first draft of the manuscript making helpful observations about its general 'feel', as well as wise suggestions for omissions and additions. He also made copious corrections to its appalling spelling and grammar, all of which went far beyond the normal call of friendship.

Graham Heaps, March 2018

ONE

The fulfilment of a dream

'I'd like to spend my whole life with that girl.'

STRANGE as it seems even to me, I can never remember a time when being married wasn't one of my great ambitions. Certainly by the time I arrived in *junior school* I always had to have a girlfriend in tow, though no 'conquest' ever seemed to leave me satisfied. And in the background was the ever-present, delightful thought that it would be great to be grown up because then I could be married: then I would have one special, 'for ever' friendship.

That longing continued through teenage years, though paradoxically it was both harder to admit to it and more desperate not to be part of a promising relationship. Indeed, I was envious of lads who had steady girlfriends. Others wanted to be famous, or academically successful, or simply well-heeled. I just wanted to be married. And my passion to be married matched my passions for Watford

FC, for my racing bike, and for playing bridge. And, indeed, for following Christ, for although I was brought up in a home without religion I had become a surprised and maybe even somewhat reluctant convert to Christianity just before my sixteenth birthday.

My decision to go to university was a late and half-hearted one. In the upper sixth of our local red-brick grammar school I had eventually applied for university because it seemed an easier option than looking for work. After very little thought, I decided that if I did go I would study geography.

There were three reasons for that. Firstly, I quite enjoyed it. Secondly, I was tolerably good at it. And thirdly, I was told that it was the easiest subject in which to get a degree. That was very important to a young man who tried never to exert himself when it came to school work. Incidentally, my experience when I eventually arrived in university served only to confirm the truth of the assertion concerning a geography degree!

I duly selected five provincial universities to which to apply, handed my UCCA form in to the school office for my teachers to write their comments on Graham Heaps, and waited for the offers to flood in. I quickly had a reasonable offer from the University College of Wales in Aberystwyth, but since it was the back of beyond and the British university furthest from a professional football club, I seriously considered turning it down. However, no other offers came: doubtless my teachers had commented on my poor work ethic and this had scared off Exeter, Bristol, Southampton and Keele.

Even after my A-level results had arrived, I was in two minds about whether to go to university or whether to do what I really wanted to do, namely manual outside work for the local council, on the dustbins or in the parks department. Only at the last minute did I decide to give in to the pressure from home and school and head for university. So in September 1968 I left the Home Counties' suburbia of my upbringing and headed to the mid-Wales coast with a single suitcase and no accommodation.

Upon arrival in Aberystwyth I was pointed in the direction of the college accommodation office and managed to find myself digs in a small bed and breakfast establishment. It was only a stone's throw from the sea front, and just behind the police station which has since been made famous by the TV detective drama, 'Hinterland.'

There on my very first afternoon I met Ian Anderson, a fellow Geography and Economics student who shared my passion for football and playing hockey, though he had a much more cultured taste in music than my enthusiasm for John Mayall and Jimi Hendrix! It was a gracious providence that put us together as we got on well and helped each other to muddle through the newness of university life.

Though my faith was weak and I had much to learn, I became a regular at the Christian Union on Saturday evenings. I loved the meetings and got lots out of them, although because of my shyness I always felt awkward and sometimes intensely lonely when the formal part of the meeting ended. Surprisingly I was eventually appointed assistant to the bookstall secretary, though I'd hardly ever read a book in my life, let alone a Christian book.

Gradually Christian friendships began to develop as well as ones with guys who were either on my course, in the Bridge Club or played for the second eleven at hockey. And one of those friendships proved key when, in the final days of my first year, PhD student Gwyn Davies from Ynys-y-bwl near Pontypridd, asked me if I'd like to join him, along with three other Christian students and an eccentric but kindly landlady in a house down by the harbour when the new academic year began.

It was also towards the end of my first year in Aberystwyth that I first noticed Susan Lawson. She was a rather loud, larger than life character from inner London who had started to attend the CU with some friends from Alexandra Hall. She was full of fun, had short cropped hair and was a little overweight. I found her a bit overpowering, and she was certainly not on my developing list of possibilities as far as finding a wife was concerned. Soon after I first met her I heard that she, too, had become a Christian.

And what a remarkable change came over Sue as a result of coming to Christ. By the time I'd started attending the same church as her (Alfred Place Baptist) in the middle of the autumn term, she had really begun to blossom as a Christian. She had become gentler, humbler and much less self-absorbed. She was still fun-loving and at the heart of things, but had a striking graciousness, as well as an authentic earnestness about her new found faith. She had also grown her hair, lost weight, and started to dress with a very becoming modesty. Unsurprisingly, she was beginning to turn the heads of a number of young men in the CU. Certainly mine was often turned in her direction!

I remember vividly the night I completely lost my heart to her. It was Saturday and we were at the main CU gathering in the basement of the Students' Union in Laura Place. After the meeting I was working on the bookstall when my friend Allan Lloyd asked me if I would go with him to the social gathering that usually followed the meeting. That night it was in Susan Lawson's room, in Alexandra Hall at the end of the prom. He asked me regularly, but I'm not sure I'd ever been before. Yet however shy I was, I just couldn't pass up the opportunity to be in Sue's room, and perhaps to have the joy of talking to her.

Since I had responsibility to pack away the bookstall, I guess that Allan and I were the last arrivals at Sue's room that evening. There were plenty there, but I had butterflies on being personally welcomed by Sue with her trademark smile and asked what I would like to drink. Next time I was free to notice her, she was sitting on her bed talking to a young man who had been to CU for the first time that night.

Indeed, I was near enough to her to be able to hear what she was saying. She was enthusiastically sharing her new-found faith. She was joyful and earnest, yet kindly and sympathetic. She spoke gently and listened well to his replies. I was utterly enraptured by her grace, her beauty and her Cockney accent. I could not take my eyes off her. I remember simply saying to myself, 'I want to spend the rest of my life with that girl!' I felt convinced that I had found the one I'd been longing for since childhood.

As people began to drift away from the social, Allan asked me if I'd accompany him to Borth. He was one of very few students with a car and so had offered a lift to a lass who was living out at the Librarianship hostel there. On the way back I plucked up courage to tell him of my passionate regard for pretty Miss Lawson. Allan was astonished at my openness and the intensity of my feelings. He told me that I needed to speak to her quickly as he knew that others were beginning to notice her.

I was discouraged. How could this tongue-tied introvert possibly speak to a girl who set him all in a whirl? Eventually he reminded me that I could write well, so I settled on a letter expressing my warm regard and admiration for her, and my desire to know her better.

The letter was easily written as I've never had problems expressing my feelings on paper. Yet fear of rejection and panic over how to talk articulately to Sue haunted me. Hence I spent my spare time the following day in the National Library of Wales in case the love of my life called at the house on South Road! She did! Imagine my embarrassment then to arrive back for tea to be greeted by Gwyn giving a none-too-impressive rendering of 'She's a lassie from London town' with the message that I was to ring Sue at seven o'clock that evening.

Those were days long before the advent of the mobile phone. Ringing Sue meant finding an empty public call box and having plenty of change to feed it. And ringing Alexandra Hall meant ringing one of two public phones provided there for the use of over two hundred young women. It also meant a stomach-churning cocktail of panic, hope and fear. Imagine my horror then to be told by the girl on phone duty at the other end of the line that Sue Lawson was already speaking to her mother on the other phone!

Eventually I spoke to her and we arranged to meet that very evening. We walked together the whole length of Aberystwyth sea front, just learning about each other. It was to be the first of many such walks. Reaching the harbour we sat and talked some more, before retracing our steps. I remember saying good-bye to Sue on the 'Alex' steps, and then running back to South Road, feeling happier than I had ever felt in my life.

Sue told me later that she had been shocked to receive such a letter from a Christian student, whom she had noticed only because he was the one who looked like a white version of Jimi Hendrix. Apparently she had shown the letter to two trusted Christian friends who had reassured her that, in spite of his unusual hair, Graham Heaps was a gentle, kindly, earnest, serious-minded Christian. To my astonishment they had also told her that she could do a lot worse than walk out with him! I am more thankful than I could possibly say for their support, and for her willingness to take the plunge.

Our courtship lasted almost two and a half years. For the first half of that we were in Aberystwyth together, and saw each other almost daily. We met up often during the holidays, too, for it took me only around an hour to cycle the twenty miles from my home west of Watford to Sue's parents' flat in Stamford Hill in North London. Incidentally, though Sue's family were from traditional British stock, I was fascinated to discover that Stamford Hill was, and still is, the very heart of Orthodox Judaism in Britain.

After our degrees Sue remained in Aberystwyth to be trained as a teacher while I enrolled at the South Wales Bible College in Barry. Eventually we were married at Alfred Place Baptist Church in our beloved Aberystwyth on July 8th, 1972. We were young, immature and very much in love, and so excited at last to be man and wife. But would the reality match up to my lifelong dreams?

TWO

The story of a marriage

Living the dream

FOR AN INCURABLE ROMANTIC LIKE ME, the danger in looking back over the more than forty years of our marriage is to view it all through rose-coloured spectacles. Indeed, Sue often accused me of wearing those very glasses while we were together, whenever I told her that she was beautiful or wonderful, words to which I often resorted over the years. I inevitably responded to such playful criticism with one rather oblique observation that seemed to amuse, satisfy and frustrate her in equal measure. I asked her at least to agree that I never took the spectacles off! Yet now it is important that I prise them off in order to give all my readers as honest a picture of our marriage, and of my wife, as I can.

Yet however closely and carefully I scrutinise our years together, I still end up with a sense of joy and thankfulness to the living God for the whole experience of that life of sweet companionship. To be sure there were times when all was not peace and harmony. Indeed, bouts of stubbornness and selfishness — mostly, but not exclusively, mine — did sometimes bring tension and frustration into our life together. Yet thanks to the wisdom of the biblical injunction not to 'let the sun go down on your wrath' (Ephesians 4:26), allied to the realisation that it is vital to be ready to say 'sorry' whenever it is needed, most of the time it was a delightful and hugely satisfying relationship that we shared. Indeed, I suspect it was evident to almost all who knew us well that we were literally best friends, and far more 'in love' after forty plus years of marriage than on our wedding day.

Our marriage was built squarely on the foundation of our shared Christian faith. That may seem surprising when you realise that we had both grown up in homes basically unsympathetic to Biblical religion. Yet each of us had been awakened to a conviction of the truth of the Christian faith by a combination of hearing direct, powerful preaching and seeing the wonderful effects of believing on a crucified Saviour in the lives of others. Strangely, for both of us the decision to follow Christ brought strong opposition from our fathers, though my Dad was more frustrated and Sue's more distressed. Yet since we had both tasted God's extraordinary grace we were both committed to follow whatever Christ taught and wherever he led.

It became apparent even in the early days of courtship that, besides our shared faith in a mighty, sovereign, gracious God, we had little else in common. Sue was a cultured girl who enjoyed the theatre, ballet, reading, and visiting stately homes. She also liked classical music, pop ballads and gentle love songs. She loved crowded places, talking with people and having friends come to visit. She was a very good listener, but was not very tactile.

Her home was important to her, and she loved to keep it neat and tidy. She liked to change things round from time to time, and was ready to attempt just about any decorating task. She enjoyed tasteful things and low lighting. She also loved having a garden and seeking to make it as pretty as she could. Sue had endless time for her family, and often for anyone else whom she could serve. And she just never stopped working, even though she could do more in an hour or two than anybody else I've ever met.

I, on the other hand, was habitually lazy and at the time we first met just loved both professional football and riding long distances on my bike. Sadly, Sue saw nothing remotely interesting in watching Watford FC and couldn't even ride a bike! I am still not at all cultured, unless you consider listening to blues, rock guitarists and intense classical music cultured. Sue didn't. I also like bright lights and lonely places, and can be content with my own company. I'm messy and disorganised, dislike change, and positively loathe gardening. Oh, and I loved nothing more than to hold Sue tight and often!

Yet we generally managed to share life together, and eventually even discovered the strange pleasure that comes when you enable a precious friend to do something they really enjoy. How often I was drawn into worlds that were naturally foreign to me by watching Sue's delight in them. There were limitations, of course. Sue never could never bring herself to pay to watch professional football, and I never accompanied her to the ballet!

Furthermore, although I said we had nothing in common, that was not absolutely true. We did discover a mutual pleasure in a few things, like watching 'Inspector Morse' and 'Endeavour', listening to audio books in the car or in bed, sharing a cream tea in a coffee shop, walking together hand-in-hand, and visiting the far-off seaside. Oh, and we also shared an almost pathological dislike of shopping!

The backdrop to our life together was largely the run-down, post-industrial town of Dewsbury in West Yorkshire. It was here we moved in November 1973, just sixteen months after our wedding, and here that Sue died forty-two years later in the last week of October 2015. Almost all that time I was the (first) pastor of Dewsbury Evangelical Church (DEC), a fellowship that had clearly been told how to call a pastor but clearly not how to get rid of one!

Over the years the church has been strikingly blessed by God, and we have seen many lives transformed by the message of the gospel. Where once there were six members there are now around a hundred. Also, in the mid-1980s the church successfully planted a similar one in Mirfield, three miles to the west of us, which is also now thriving. DEC is now seeking to do the same in the Lupset and Flanshaw area of the city of Wakefield, some six miles to the east of Dewsbury.

Sue's number one anxiety in coming north to Dewsbury was that she would be expected to fill a definite role of leadership among women in the church, for which she felt totally unfitted. Indeed, I had to reassure her that in my eyes her main task was simply to be my wife and the maker and keeper of our modest home. She was never comfortable at the front of any kind of meeting, though she was quite capable of being there. Yet she gradually and very naturally gained a significant place in the church as an encourager, helper and friend to most. In so doing, and without ever realising it, she provided a real example of cheerful, servant-hearted womanhood to many.

One of her greatest assets was her serious commitment to keep all confidences shared with her. As a result she was not only sought out by many for advice about all things to do with running a home and looking after children, but for wisdom and support in times of personal crisis. I only have begun to grasp the scale of Sue's ministry in those very private areas since her death, as friends have expressed grief at losing her readiness to listen and her wise counsel that so helped them with difficult situations of which I often knew nothing.

A large part of the reason why Sue was regarded as a fount of wisdom on matters relating to bringing up children was undoubtedly the fact that, during the first thirteen years of our marriage, the Lord blessed us with no less than five children, two boys and then three girls. As I like to quip, we were two up at half time and lost three-two! In truth, ours was a conscious decision to have a big family if we could, a choice that neither of us ever regretted. Mind, there were times when the children were teenagers when even Sue's legendary patience was exposed as impatience and our parenting skills were shown to be very limited indeed.

Sue was in her element as a mother. From day one she was unusually competent as well as confident, no doubt drawing on her experience of helping her elder sister Jean with her children in earlier years. She mostly coped well with the huge workload involved, often with very little help from her husband whose own workload as pastor of a growing church was also considerable.

It has to be admitted that there were times when the marriage became rather stale from the sheer lack of time we were spending together, but in our late thirties the relationship was revitalised in a very unusual way. I started to teach Sue to drive! To many that claim will seem unbelievable, for marriages have often been put under great strain by such foolhardiness. But for us, the hours spent on Tuesday and Thursday afternoons in the car park behind our church building on Crackenedge Lane while Sue learned to steer a car, and to control it using the clutch and gear lever, were very precious times of re-kindling a romance.

In truth, we just needed those hours together, stolen from incredibly busy schedules: just the two of us, away from the kids. It gave me the chance to be gentle, kind, patient and supportive. It also forced me to notice that, in spite of having had five children, Sue was still a stunningly attractive woman. And I realised then, probably for the first time, it was for my sake that she continued to make considerable efforts with her appearance.

Life as the pastor's wife and mother to his five children meant not only that Sue was very busy, but also that she was far from wealthy! Yet she remained as cheerful as ever, and never once complained about how little we had. Indeed, she showed real ability to stretch our meagre resources, plus a willingness to supplement the family income by taking on cleaning duties for (often elderly) friends. Most of those for whom she worked were shocked by the speed with which she could clean and tidy a room or a bungalow, or strip and re-make a bed, or get through a basket of ironing.

Interestingly, too, when in later years we did have a little more money Sue took great pleasure in giving most of the extra away, responding in delighted generosity to pretty well every case of particular need in her wide circle of friends and acquaintances of which she heard. There have been quite a few occasions when I have been approached at the end of a service by a beaming member of the congregation who was wanting to thank me for my liberality — about which I had to confess to knowing nothing at all! But Sue's often spontaneous generosity gave me great joy, and provided me with yet another excuse to go home, take her in my arms and tell her of the pleasure I found in so much of what she did.

One of the things that I found most pleasing and surprising about Sue was her willingness to take so much of the domestic work off my shoulders. She was not only the family chef and shopper, but the chief decorator and gardener too. As I've hinted before, she was also in charge of the money. In addition she arranged the family holidays and packed everything to take on them, generally including her husband's suitcase! Occasionally she complained about having to think of plans for my days off or to arrange for a repair man to come, but generally she did everything, and did it cheerfully.

Another thing that made her a joy to live with was her unusual ability to laugh at herself. Most of us take ourselves far too seriously. Not so my Sue. It meant that she was very difficult to offend. Indeed, the occasions when she got really upset with others were so rare that they stand out as a few very 'out of character moments' in a life time of memories of a lady characterised by a beautiful smile and an infectious laugh.

Hence forty plus years of married bliss passed in a flash, and we began to think about my retirement from 'the ministry'. Together we decided that I needed to stop at sixty-five. I still loved the work, but was weary, having worked sixty-plus hours a week for decades. Indeed, I had only been able to continue in the work for as long as I had because not long after I reached sixty the church called my friend Daniel Grimwade to work alongside me.

From day one Daniel showed that he was ready to do so much more than simply help me in the work, and with my encouragement and to my delight he became 'the main man' under Christ in the church. As a result I was able to press on towards sixty five, and also to begin to plan with Sue for a new life beyond the pastorate that been my preoccupation for so long. Yet our plans were about to be torn up in spectacular fashion by the God of providence.

THREE

The fateful diagnosis

Sudden storm clouds in a blue sky

ON SUNDAY NOVEMBER 16TH 2014, Susan Heaps, my precious wife of forty-three years, was diagnosed at Dewsbury District Hospital with a large, multi-headed brain tumour requiring urgent surgery. And within days we were warned by a consultant at Leeds General Infirmary that it was likely to lead to her death, and that the brutal operation that faced her was ultimately only palliative, holding out the hope of extending her life for up to four years at best.

It was a diagnosis for which we had had almost no warning. We had noticed symptoms of a problem for only a few days at the most. The first thing that had struck me was that Sue was driving unusually close to the kerb, but I put it down to the fact that she wasn't used to driving our 'main' car which was wider than her beloved Nissan Micra. Indeed, she scratched the Honda Jazz on a 'road works' sign, having never before scratched any car in twenty-five years of driving.

Later in the week she began to have difficulties with getting out of the chair and the bath, and when she fell out of bed on Saturday evening (and we had quite a pantomime getting her up again) I wanted to take her to A & E. She settled instead for reading her medical book and we both realised that the problem must be in her head. It was only after the diagnosis that she admitted she had thought then that she must have a brain tumour, but she didn't want to worry me with that idea at the time just in case she was wrong.

This was almost the first time in her life that Sue had ever been poorly. All our married life she had been the healthy one, whereas I had had a series of very occasional health scares from peritonitis to transient global amnesia to suspected heart attacks (which turned out to be gastric problems) to ventricular tachycardia. Whereas I had been in an emergency ambulance with lights flashing and sirens blaring on at least five occasions, Sue had never been in hospital overnight, apart from following the birth of each of our children.

Yet here was the concerned casualty doctor telling Sue, me and our GP friend Deborah (who had kindly taken Sue to hospital that Sunday morning while I went to DEC to preach) that the CT scan had revealed a large tumour at the front of her brain. It was as if a totally un-forecast storm had blown up in a cloudless sky to disturb the beautiful early autumn of our lives.

In truth, though, I should have anticipated that this day might eventually come. Why so? Well, already three members of Sue's nuclear family had been struck by the dreaded cancer. Her father had had an operation to remove his bowel in his early sixties. Her mum had died of inoperable ovarian cancer aged sixty-nine. And her elder sister, Jean, had died of breast cancer at the young age of fifty-two. Sue herself had had scares regarding cancer in her late forties when a routine test revealed that one of her ovaries was enlarged. Eventually the powers that be concluded that it had probably always been so, just as some folk are born with one foot bigger than the other!

Nevertheless, in spite of all the potential warning signs I had never dreamed that Sue might die before me. After all, women live longer than men, and I was the one whose 'heart electrics' were somewhat 'dodgy'. Very remarkably, only five days earlier I had been examined at Pinderfields Hospital in Wakefield by a brain specialist to make sure that a severe but 'painless' migraine incident I had experienced some days before that was not caused by a brain tumour! And here was my always healthy Sue terminally ill with the same condition.

However, though the diagnosis was utterly unexpected in a woman who had always enjoyed fabulous health, it gradually dawned on us that our gracious heavenly Father had been preparing us for a while to face that alarming day.

And recognising the unmistakable fact of that preparation has been a great encouragement to me both then and since.

The way the Lord got Sue ready to face her ordeal was very striking. Just a couple of years earlier she had read and reviewed a book that had revolutionised her view of the future and brought her to realise for the very first time that heaven really was something to which she could look forward with great anticipation. That book, by American pastor Randy Alcorn, is simply called *Heaven*.

The focus of Alcorn's study is not so much the temporary world into which the Christian passes at death. His main emphasis, like that of the New Testament itself, is on the promise of the return of Christ and the resurrection of the dead. He trawls the Bible for every detail we are there given about that life. He shows clearly that we will live in a gloriously solid, three-dimensional world, like this one only delivered from its bondage to decay, and free of all that frustrates and brings pain.

The way that book changed Sue's outlook on the future is plain from the review of it that she wrote in 2012. Among her comments is this telling, almost frustrated, aside: 'I realise that I cannot, by this brief review, convey to you the delight and excitement with which the writer has infected me concerning the world to come!' But its effect on her was clear from the fact that on a number of occasions in her final days Sue asked Matthew, our elder son, to read her a chapter or two from that book in order to fill and excite her mind again with thoughts of that world that would one day be hers.

Shortly after Sue's diagnosis I started to realise that the Lord had also been preparing me for coping with the trauma of her condition and the prospect of losing her. That realisation brought wonderful reassurance that I was not on my own in this greatest trial of my life, and that the divine Shepherd would walk with me in the gloomy 'valley of the shadow of death.' That preparation had taken at least two evident forms.

First of all, a couple of years earlier, I had been deeply moved by reading in John 11 the account of Jesus's reaction to the death of his dear friend Lazarus. By turns John shows us Jesus's great confidence in his power to overcome death, his anger and outrage in the face of death (somewhat obscured in many translations, but clear in the original), and his great compassion and sensitivity towards the bereaved sisters, Martha and Mary. The effect on me was such that I eventually decided to prepare a sermon on the passage under the sobering title, 'A Christian view of death.'

I preached that sermon in three or four places, each time with unusual effect. But it was the deepening of my own understanding of death, and of my emotional reactions to it, that were the really lasting results. Throughout Sue's suffering, and since her death, I have felt comfortable both in despising death and yet knowing a deep confidence that Christ has truly conquered it for my dear one.

The other very marked way that the Lord had got me ready to cope with the shocking news of Sue's large brain tumour was again in the realm of my own reflections on what to preach. As my retirement date was set for December 31st, 2014, the beginning of November brought the commencement of my final sermon series as minister of Dewsbury Evangelical Church. I remember having more than usual difficulty in settling on a theme for that last endeavour to bring God's word to bear on 'my people' as their pastor. I knew there would probably be plenty of opportunities to preach there again, but wanted to mark the end of an era for all at the church with something of truly lasting value.

In the end I decided to do something I could not remember having done before: to rework a series I had already preached in the church. More than ten years earlier I had felt great help in preparing ministry on God as the Father of every one who believes in his Son, inspired by Sinclair Ferguson's splendid little book, *Children of the Living God*. It was a series of sermons that had been much appreciated, and had been used by God to bring at least one person to new life in Christ, and I was confident that it could be widely useful again in the significantly changed congregation if I gave myself to preparing it afresh before the Lord. That confidence was reinforced by my conviction that I had grown in my own understanding and experience of that fatherly care in the years since I had first preached on the theme. What I didn't realise was that no one would need its deeply reassuring truths in the days ahead more than the preacher himself.

Indeed, so appropriate did I find it, and so strengthening to my soul, that I preached on the fatherhood of God not only on the morning that Deborah came to examine Sue and take her to Casualty, but also on the following Sunday, the day before Sue's brain surgery in Leeds, while Sue stayed at home with our middle daughter, Jo. And so great was my need of the ballast to my soul provided by the realisation that in Christ God had become my heavenly Father that I laid down my series only very reluctantly in order to focus absolutely on my beloved helpmeet and her needs.

In fact, to my shame, it took a visit from Colin Mountain, my friend, companion and unfailingly faithful supporter throughout the adventure that has been Dewsbury Evangelical Church, to make me see that I must not keep going with the preaching work, however greatly I needed the truths that I was planning to share. Not for the first time I needed to face the fact that my elders were wiser than I, this time in seeing that the Lord himself had decreed an earlier date for my retirement than Sue and I had planned. But I run ahead of myself. I need to return to the events following the day of the dreaded diagnosis.

FOUR

Under the Knife

Surgery and the immediate aftermath

AFTER THE DIAGNOSIS things moved ahead rapidly. Sue was immediately admitted to Ward 6 at Dewsbury District Hospital. At first she seemed both alarmingly disorientated and very fearful of what lay ahead, especially the pain. And for those of us who were looking on, the almost overnight transformati on from her normal, healthy, articulate self to this stumbling confused lady was deeply distressing and seemed full of foreboding. Yet even then our alarms were quickly tempered by the kindness of our covenant God.

In his sweet providence, Ward 6 was at that time served by a dear young Asian friend of Sue's called Reumah. Having her around was a great source of encouragement to Sue. On top of that very personal blessing, her immediate problems with balance and confusion were quickly overcome by a dose of steroids and she was soon more her old self. Indeed, by late morning on Wednesday Sue was well enough to accompany me by taxi to see the consultant at Leeds General Infirmary. However, that trip illustrated the organisational inefficiency that so often plagues the NHS, for Sue met the brain specialist a few hours *before* Dewsbury District Hospital had got around to scheduling an MRI scan of her brain!

We were well treated at LGI. The consultant, Mr Sivakumar, answered all our questions with realism and sensitivity. The planned operation was explained, as well as its severe limitations. Mr Sivakumar offered his firm, soon to be confirmed, opinion that the tumour was primary and fast-growing, and would prove to be the highest grade of cancer. His aim in the operation would be to remove as much of the growth as possible, and so relieve the pressure on the brain as well as providing material to confirm exactly what we were dealing with. But he warned us that he would not be able to remove it all because of its tentacle-like structure.

As a result, the consultant indicated that Sue would need both chemotherapy and radiotherapy when she had recovered from the surgery. However, he expressed his confidence that the operation and subsequent treatment would significantly lengthen Sue's life from the perhaps six months that she was likely to survive without any intervention. He also held out the hope of every likelihood of a good quality to whatever life remained to her, and assured her that she need expect to be in hospital no more than about two to three weeks after the operation.

We returned to Dewsbury by taxi, hand in hand, in time for the promised MRI scan, and the following day Sue was discharged until Sunday afternoon. Then she would need to be taken back to LGI in readiness for the operation that had been fixed for Monday morning. The continuation of the steroids meant that Sue was pretty well back to normal by Friday, and I can remember holding hands and talking on Saturday evening, as we had done so many times before.

As I looked at her my mind was flooded with pride in how this dear woman had coped with all the shock and trauma of the past week. I wondered if Sue would express a desire for the gentle intimacy of making love, as she had sometimes done before when she was seeking comfort in times of great anxiety. However, she seemed very content just to have me close to her, seeking to reassure her that our faithful God would be at her side in all that lay ahead. Little did I realise then that never again would she be well enough to enable us to express our love and commitment to each other in that fitting, beautiful, intimate, God-given way.

As I explained earlier, the next morning this stubborn man went off to preach on a passage of Scripture that had been such a blessing to me through the week that I couldn't bear to forgo the opportunity to share my treasure with others. I learned later how open to sad misunderstanding this was when one visitor to the church commented on how cruel the fellowship must be to force the minister to leave his wife the day before a life-changing operation in order to fulfil his contractual obligation to preach!

That afternoon I drove Sue to LGI and she was admitted to a single pre-op room. We talked and prayed, and I eventually headed home, promising to return in the morning in the hope of seeing her before she was taken down to theatre. We both slept surprisingly well in response to fervent prayer.

We were both very thankful that the operation was a little delayed in the morning and I was indeed able to sit, pray and read the Bible with Sue before she was summoned for surgery. Around noon I walked beside Sue's bed as it was rolled through the hospital to the doors of the theatre corridor. There I squeezed her hand and kissed her face, and left her in the hands of competent strangers and our covenant God. After that there followed what seemed like the longest nine hours of my life.

What do you do while another man has his hands inside your wife's skull and is chopping away at what he finds there with a knife? That is probably a libellous description of what was going on in theatre, but it was how I imagined it at the time. Well, I wandered somewhat aimlessly around central Leeds, bought a 'meal deal' from WH Smith's, and sat on a bench to eat, read my New Testament and pray — all the while lost in a sea of humanity. After that I perused a model railway magazine I had bought and then browsed all manner of interesting books in Waterstones. Time seemed almost to stand still.

Eventually around 16.30 I received a phone call from our youngest daughter, Chloe, to say that the surgeon had been trying to get hold of me. I remember carefully pressing in the digits of the number given to me and waiting tensely for the news. How grateful I was to hear that it was very positive. Sue had come through the operation and was now resting in the recovery area. Mr Sivakumar was pleased with what he had been able to do, and suggested that I went quickly to the visitors' room in Ward 24 to await Sue's arrival on the ward, which he anticipated would be in half an hour or so.

How wrong he was! In truth it was to be a good four hours before I would have the joy of seeing my beloved, swathed in bandages and looking rather groggy. The delays were quite natural and not medically significant. Sue slept more deeply than usual after the operation and things were very busy on Ward 24, so it was a while before she could be brought up. Then nobody remembered to tell her anxious husband that she was now on the ward!

Yet those were very strange and disturbing hours for me, and quite a bit of their strangeness had nothing at all to do with my Sue. Sure, I remember feeling increasingly anxious because I had heard nothing and nobody seemed able to tell me what was going on. But my anxiety was increased by the fact that I was losing my voice to a throat infection. Not only did I muse on whether they would let me spend all the time I wanted to with Sue if I evidently had an infection, but I was confronted by a situation in the sitting room where I was with which I desperately wanted to help, but couldn't because my voice was so weak.

There was an eastern European family there who had brought in a neighbour's teenage daughter for investigation after some kind of fit. They all seemed very agitated and distressed by the situation, and though their English was limited I felt an overwhelming desire to offer to pray with them for the Lord's help in their situation. Yet I didn't even have sufficient voice for that task, let alone to be able tell them of my experience of the Lord's tenderness to all who seek him in truth.

Eventually I heard a bed being moved on the corridor and went out to find Sue being wheeled from a side room to a place near the nursing station, as the consultant had decreed that while she didn't require a bed in Intensive Care she did need to be watched constantly for the next day or two. Sue seemed sleepy but the wide smile was recognisably hers and she looked surprisingly well. As a result I made my way home feeling at peace and with a deep sense of gratitude in my heart. Little did I realise that Sue would still be at LGI seven weeks later, having seemingly made very little progress in all that time.

And so began a strange new life for us both. For Sue it was the routine of life in hospital, learning to cope not only with pain, sickness and immobility, but also with unexpectedly slow progress. For me it was an equally strange new world. My mornings consisted of shopping, household duties, writing emails and answering the phone. Then it was time for a quick lunch and a brisk walk to the railway station as my own earlier visit to hospital had brought the instruction not to drive for at least a month in case the diagnosis was faulty.

The eleven-minute train ride was followed by a brisk

half-mile walk to the hospital and the 'bounce' up six flights of stairs. Then I was allowed to spend a full six hours talking to Sue and seeing to her needs. These included serving her the hotel quality food and doing all the little things that made her more comfortable. I was also there to entertain her many visitors as we were overwhelmed by the sheer number of people who came to see and encourage Sue. Finally it was an affectionate farewell at eight, followed by a hasty dash downhill to the station in the hope of getting home as early as possible for my evening meal.

Those evening meals were among the most delightful blessings of the whole time Sue was in hospital. One friend or another from the church daily provided me with a feast that I simply needed to pop into the microwave on arrival at home. They were unfailingly tasty and nourishing meals and the most vividly tangible reminder of the love of a congregation desperate for good news of Sue.

Within a week or so my daughter-in-law Rachel suggested that it would be easier for me if I ate these wonderful offerings at their house so she could have them piping hot on the table as soon as I walked in. Those meals, plus the large numbers of church people who took the trouble of visiting Sue at the hospital, were a real demonstration of the bonds the Spirit of Christ has formed in our church, and of the practical love and service that are a beautiful feature of life there.

FIVE

Dark days at LGI

Pain and peace in the daunting valley

IT WAS no surprise to any of us that Sue was weak, weary and in considerable pain after the drastic surgery. However, it was a profound shock to see that six weeks later she was not only still in hospital, but still unable to stand even with a Zimmer frame and still being horrendously sick every time they got her out of bed or attempted to give her any exercise to perform. Indeed, it was obvious to all that in some ways her medical condition had deteriorated since the operation.

At first Sue had seemed to be making steady, if rather slow, progress. After a few days she was awake most of the time, even though she mostly kept her eyes closed as the light troubled her. Furthermore, in spite of needing me to spoon-feed her, she was eating well, doubtless helped by the wonderfully appetising meals that were being provided for her. And she had begun to respond very positively to the many visitors who came to see her.

Yet it was a shock to see that even after more than a fortnight she still could not move her left hand at all, let alone lift it off the bed. She also continued to have significant levels of pain in her head, neck and back, and oral morphine became a regular part of her medication.

Gradually conversations with the staff became less optimistic. They spoke lots about her urgent need to begin treatment — both chemotherapy and radiotherapy — but always underlined that she would need to be very much stronger before it could start. Talk of her coming home soon died away, and they encouraged me to try to work with her by moving her left hand. It seemed like a hopeless task until one glorious day I caught her scratching her nose - a powerful demonstration that the problem was in her brain and not in the muscles of her arm.

Yet in spite of the gradual recovery of strength to her left arm and hand, other distressing physical symptoms remained and even intensified. Kind staff made heroic efforts to help Sue to stand, at least with a frame, but Sue's determination to make progress just brought fearful bouts of vomiting that clearly shocked even the most experienced of the nursing staff. She became still more weak and weary even though she continued to eat well. As a result the children and I found it increasingly difficult to retain any optimism regarding the future.

However, through it all Sue, though sometimes very discouraged herself, continued to show great courage and patience. Indeed, we had lovely times together, chatting and holding hands. In truth, she was probably the most kissed patient Ward 24 has ever had! And except when she was feeling horrible pain or lots of nausea she just loved to see her visitors, especially those who prayed with her and sought to stimulate and strengthen her faith in the Good Shepherd.

One particular friend of mine, Alan Liu, happened to work in that area of the hospital, and regularly called to see Sue outside normal visiting hours. Each time he came he brought little gifts of food or hand cream from his wife Rachel, and always sought to encourage Sue with verses of Scripture. Occasionally, on an afternoon when Sue had other visitors, I would call at his office and our times of prayer together were very precious. One thing that greatly helped Sue through these tough times was the kindness of all the staff who worked on Ward 24. They were unfailingly attentive and thoughtful, and genuinely upset by Sue's lack of progress. Sinead, her main physiotherapist, bought her expensive chocolates at Christmas and was visibly distressed at her inability to help Sue to make the progress we all wanted to see. One young nurse even bought Sue a vibrating neck cushion with her own money in the hope that it might relieve some of the pain and tension she was experiencing in that area.

Around the turn of the year things reached rock bottom as I began to get advice that I needed to find a nursing home in Dewsbury to which Sue could be transferred from LGI. I was gently told that she would be very unlikely ever to be able to be at home again, and that a nursing home would be the best place for her for the few weeks or months that remained to her in this world. It was a truly devastating assessment for us both, but it seemed the only possible way ahead in view of her poor and deteriorating state of health. The only slight reason for any hope on the medical front was that she had been diagnosed with a virulent infection in her stomach which they were now treating with strong antibiotics, in the hope that they might reduce her chronic nausea.

You will easily grasp just how discouraging that time was for me if I tell you that at the beginning of Sue's ordeal I had been wondering whether our glorious God might heal her miraculously. I was certainly confident that such a thing could happen, as I had seen some very striking answers to prayer over the years, including in the realm of healing. So, from the day of diagnosis, seeking healing had been one aspect of my prayer for Sue, alongside a passionate desire that she might gain a deeper knowledge of her Lord and trust in him through whatever came her way. Yet we had received no indication whatever that it was the Lord's intention to heal her. Indeed, now even the dream of having her at home so that I could nurse, support and pamper her seemed hopeless.

Yet all through this heartache, and to my profound surprise, I found myself enjoying a deep peace of heart and even a strange kind of contentment bordering on joy for many hours every single day. And so, for the first time in my life, I not only realised the profound truth of the Bible's promise of real peace for those who cast their burdens on the Lord, but I also grasped that it is those who *experience* that peace who are the ones who are most convinced that (in the apostle Paul's words) it is 'beyond understanding' or 'utterly inexplicable' (Philippians 4:6-7). I was certainly as bemused as I was grateful for the experience!

Doubtless a whole range of blessings contributed to my sense of joy in the lowest days of Sue's ordeal. One was the extraordinary love, kindness and sympathy I was shown by so many people. Our children and their spouses were unfailingly thoughtful and supportive, even though their hearts were breaking, too. Those who lived locally came very regularly to the hospital to visit their mum, often accompanied by their spouses and their youngsters. And those who lived far away made heroic efforts to visit as often as possible. How it delighted Sue to see her grandchildren, all thirteen of them, though on her worst days she hardly seemed aware that they were there.

In addition, members of our extended family and friends from afar constantly rang or sent emails, cards and letters expressing love and good wishes. Sue poured over every card and eagerly enquired for news of those who had contacted me by phone or electronically. On top of all this, people queued up to visit Sue and none seemed offended to be told when to come or even that they could not visit while she was so poorly.

Yet supremely it was the knowledge that literally hundreds were praying daily for the Lord to help and strengthen us all that constantly buoyed my heart.

Furthermore, past experience of my failure to be able to encourage myself with such things brought home to me that the deep peace of heart I was experiencing was truly God's doing.

Around the turn of the year I was given the profound encouragement of another very tangible proof that many people from near and far loved Sue and were desperate to help and cheer her. It all flowed from a chance remark she had made to our daughter-in-law, Rachel. Sue had mused that it would be nice to have a bright blanket to wrap around herself when she was sitting out in her wheelchair in the ward lounge. That set Rachel to thinking that many of Sue's friends would love the opportunity to do a little something for her. And so the plan was hatched.

Rachel was already helping me by sometimes writing the regular updates that I was sending out to keep people informed of Sue's progress or lack of it. One day a few lines were added to our news to ask people who could manage it to knit a square in 'double knitting' wool, measuring 20cm by 20cm, and send it to Rachel as soon as possible.

The response was quite overwhelming. One email from Christine Tyler, a friend of Sue's in the south, typified the reaction of many. She wrote, 'As an old school friend of Sue's I am deeply saddened by the onset of Sue's illness. As I live in London I have been feeling really helpless in not knowing what I could do to help cheer her up and also letting her know how much she means to me (as she will do to so very many others). It was a real delight to receive a copy of your email requesting knitted squares and I shall certainly get my knitting needles in action.'

By the time all the squares were in from more than eighty knitters, Rachel and her team of willing helpers from the church were able to make one full-size blanket and no less than six lap blankets from the 262 squares. They were an immense encouragement to Sue (and me) and a wonderfully vivid demonstration of the love and regard in which she was held by so many. In truth that very tangible support was one highly significant way in which the living God sustained a very positive spirit in both of us.

SIX

Life in the goldfish bowl

Seeking to make a mark for the Lord

OVER THE WEEKS that Sue was struggling in LGI I gradually came to realise that I was more and more living in a goldfish bowl — under the scrutiny of a great crowd of people. Staff at the hospital seemed intrigued by the appreciative man who was often seen reading the Bible to his distressingly poorly wife whom he so evidently loved deeply. They also noticed and commented on the fact that neither of us ever seemed depressed.

At the same time our five children were watching me intensely, very concerned about how their Dad was coping with their Mum's suffering. They knew that their mother was, and had always been, the delight of his life, and by a country mile the closest and most precious of his many friends. So they were very anxious as to how I would cope with this living nightmare.

People in the church also looked on tenderly, longing that I might show, in my buffeted, uncertain and tear-stained life, the authentic outworking of the truth they had heard me preach for so many years. They were desperate to see that promises of God, which had so often excited me in preaching, were now sustaining my soul, giving me evident help and hope.

Many other believers eagerly read and turned to prayer every detail that I recorded in the emails I sent out about Sue's progress or lack of it. And I knew that they looked in hope not only for better news of the patient but also for evidence that my heart was being sustained by the grace and peace of God.

News of Sue's condition also quickly reached many relatives and friends who didn't share our faith. These longed just as much to hear better news of Sue, and rode the roller coaster of hope and despair with us. Yet it became evident that some of these were also intrigued to see whether my trust in the Good Shepherd would hold up. They looked on to discover if that faith would yield any benefit to us in the trial. Would we in fact see striking 'answers' to our prayers? Would we show singularly different attitudes to our troubles from others they knew who had experienced similar things? In fact I knew that some, perhaps many, were looking on to see if there was really anything supernatural in this Christianity of ours.

It was all rather strange. I had just retired from a very public position to sit, often alone, at the bedside of my terminally ill wife. As far as prominence in the church was concerned I was very much taking a back seat. Indeed, I had given up all 'public ministry.' And yet as the weeks of our ordeal went by I became increasingly aware of my responsibility to be something attractive for the Lord in a very different kind of 'public performance.'

The result was that I found I was praying for myself with an urgency and intensity that I had probably never known before. What I needed from the Lord was that he would more than sustain in me the peace, trust, submission, hope and even joy that I had experienced in some measure since the day that Sue's dreadful tumour had been discovered. I knew that all those things were appropriate for me as his child in this, the toughest experience of my life. I knew, too, that only he could preserve and deepen these God-honouring graces in me.

During that time two passages from the Bible really held my spiritual life together. One gave strength and confidence to my feeble faith, while the other helped me greatly in the vital task of praying intelligently for myself. The first was from Luke's account of Jesus and his apostles in an upstairs room in Jerusalem the night before he was crucified. The second was from the book of Psalms in the Old Testament. So helpful were those passages to me that I was delighted to get the opportunity, even during Sue's illness, to preach on both of them to the church we had served together for generations.

Before Sue's brain tumour began to grow — and her consultant believed that it probably took only six weeks to grow from nothing to dominate the whole front right portion of the brain — I had planned to retire on the last day of 2014. To mark that occasion the church had kindly organised a special Saturday afternoon service in early December to which many people had been invited. However, as soon as Sue's condition was known that service was cancelled and later replaced by a special evening service on Sunday December 28th.

With some three weeks to contemplate the occasion I informed my co-pastor Daniel that I would like to preach at the service. I also determined that Sue's illness should not be 'the elephant in the room', but freely spoken about. Accordingly I decided to preach on the words of Jesus to the foolishly self-confident Simon Peter of which I had drunk deeply through the past few, disturbing weeks, and which had done so much to encourage and support my trust in my Saviour, Jesus Christ.

Here are the words. 'Simon, Simon, Satan has asked to sift you all as wheat; but I have prayed (very particularly) for you, Simon, that your faith may *not* fail. And when you have turned back, strengthen your brothers.' You can find those words in verses 31 and 32 of Luke chapter 22.

They are words that profoundly expressed both my situation and my confidence, both my danger and my security. They remind us of what I knew deep in my soul, namely that the best of believers is very weak and open to the assaults of the evil one. Indeed, we face the danger that the very faith that joins us to Christ and so brings us acceptance with God may be swept away with disastrous consequences. Jesus himself underlined to Peter just how real that danger is, especially in times of deep and unexpected trials.

Yet here, too, is the assurance that, through the effective prayers of the Saviour for his flawed followers, that danger is nullified. He sees and knows our terrible vulnerability, often made worse by Peter-like complacency, and overcomes it by fervent and heartfelt prayer. That was where my soul had come to rest, and so that was what I sought to share with the large congregation before me, people united by the most tender concern for Sue and me, as many conversations afterwards made very apparent.

The other passage that really strengthened my soul at that time can be found in section ten of the longest of all the Psalms, Psalm 119. In most Bibles these verses are headed by the Hebrew letter 'yodh', for in the original language each of the eight verses in the section (verses 73-80) begins with a word starting with that letter.

Here I found help in the vital business of understanding what I myself needed most from God and how to articulate it succinctly in prayer. This Psalmist, who knew what it was to be afflicted (see verses 71 and 75), taught me three great requests that I quickly made my own as I laid my personal needs before the living God in the closing year of Sue's life. These petitions brought focus and clarity to the way I prayed for myself in this time of great heartache.

First of all, I prayed that the 'unfailing love' of my covenant God would be 'my comfort' (verse 76). I was overjoyed to be reminded that God's compassion had been my birth-right since I was born again of God's Spirit as a wayward teenager. *Secondly,* I prayed that in the midst of all the trauma and upheaval of my so changed life I might not forget God's law and its wise rules for my life (verse 80). In fact, I was brought by the Psalmist to realise the danger I faced in this trial of becoming so self-absorbed that I excused all manner of personal sin. *Finally,* I began to pray that I might be able so to cope with all that was facing me that I might be a real encouragement to other believers who were looking on (verse 74).

I prayed like this because I knew that without God's mighty help I would never be able to maintain a spirit of calmness, trust and obedience to him through whatever life threw at me. I knew, too, that pretending to know peace, or joy, or dependence on the Lord, or trusting submission to his providence, would be worse than useless. I would never be able to carry it off — you just can't fake the peace of God — and God would never bless it. And I believe that these prayers were answered abundantly. I was sustained in good heart and a generally cheerful spirit. For the first time in my life I was enabled to live a day at a time without always worrying about the future. And I never felt angry with God or very low in spirits.

Needless to say, however, while Sue remained in hospital she was the number one focus of my prayers and my great concern every waking hour. Day after day I carefully chose a brief Bible passage to read to her, always seeking, with God's help, to reinforce her under-pressure faith. And many times most days I prayed fervently for her, and often with her, supremely that her faith would not fail, but that God would make her a blessing to all who came into contact with her.

Did God hear those prayers? I believe that he did, and abundantly so. And what is my evidence for that momentous claim? Well, I have to testify that in all my fifty years as a Christian I have never had so many openings, and certainly never so many requests, to share my faith and talk of the reality of God's sustaining of his wayward child, as I did in the long weeks I spent visiting on Ward 24. And so many of those opportunities came as the result of Sue's patience, cheerfulness and thankfulness. Yet all the while she lay in the corner bed in the bay across from the nursing station, making nothing like the progress that the doctors and nurses were looking and hoping for.

SEVEN

Progress at last

Off to rehab, and home, praise God!

It was on January 6th 2015, at a meeting with her consultant Mr Sivakumar, that Sue received the first positive health news in a very long time. Indeed, there were no less than three doses of cheer. First of all, a recent CT scan showed no signs whatever of further growth in the tumour. This meant that her present physical problems were not, as some staff evidently feared, signs of rapid progress of the cancer through her brain. Secondly, our friendly consultant was very confident that the recently started course of antibiotics would soon overcome the infection that he believed was at the root of her terrible nausea and vomiting. And thirdly, and most surprising of all, Mr Sivakumar believed that now was the time to send Sue for a course of rehabilitation.

In the wonderful providence of God the unit that would undertake this had recently moved from Wakefield to

Dewsbury, half a mile from our home. Better still, it was a unit in which Mr Sivakumar had great confidence. Apparently he knew and regarded highly Dr Kemp, the lady in charge of the department, and he told us that she had assembled a team who had gained a great reputation for getting people back on their feet. To us it seemed too good to be true.

On the down side, it was immediately obvious to me that some of the nursing staff who were also present at that meeting were far from sharing the consultant's heartening optimism. I was even conscious of two caring, senior staff members rolling their eyes as this consultant spoke so positively about likely outcomes. They had worked with Sue every day and had seen how poorly she had been over Christmas and New Year. Mr Sivakumar, on the other hand, had been on holiday throughout that period, and had not witnessed her decline. Yet, to our considerable surprise and great joy, the optimism of the consultant proved to be well-placed.

Four days later Sue was indeed transferred to the Stroke and Brain Injury Rehabilitation Unit on the top floor of the Bronte Tower at Dewsbury District Hospital. Ironically, it was a ward in which Sue had previously nursed at least one of her new-borns, all of whom made their first appearance in this world in Bronte Tower!

In typical NHS fashion the confirmation of the imminent move came without warning on the Saturday morning. As a result, I had no real opportunity to sort out any of the accumulated possessions that had arrived at LGI over the seven weeks of Sue's life there. In the end I had to leave it to friends to clear out the side room into which she had been moved around Christmas time in the hope of improving her sleep.

As I raced to Leeds in order to accompany Sue on her ambulance journey to Dewsbury my mind was filled with many questions and not a little foreboding. How could a woman who couldn't even stand unaided with a frame possibly engage in significant rehabilitation? How could she attempt anything like this without the dreadful sickness returning? Would she get less personal care and attention now she was moving from a flagship university hospital to an NHS backwater? In truth I was beginning to feel rather ill at ease about the whole decision.

However, the move would prove an almost unimaginable and literally breath-taking success. Within three weeks of beginning rehab Sue was able to come home, to sit up by herself, to walk with a frame, and even to negotiate safely our steep flight of stairs! All this our gracious God did for us, in response to the fervent prayers of literally hundreds of well-wishers, through the dedication of the rehab team and Sue's own determination and courage.

Sue coped well with the move itself, though she seemed a little disappointed to be put in a room with three elderly stroke patients. She was also rather frustrated when it became apparent that Ward 4 was the end of the line as far as catering was concerned. That meant she was pretty well forced to eat two stodgy main meals a day. The staff involved were used to dealing with patients with a poor appetite and difficulty with eating, and sadly would not let me supply Sue with her own much lighter lunches.

However, whatever the disappointments of Ward 4, from the first hour she arrived there and the ward sister sang the praises of the talents and kindness of the rehab team, Sue's spirit seemed to lift. From that moment on I had no doubt that she would give her all to do whatever was asked of her and more, whatever it cost her in terms of effort or pain.

On the Monday I was delighted to witness that Sue had already mastered the Rotor Stand, by which she could transfer herself from her bed to a wheelchair. By Tuesday she was not only standing without needing others to hold her up, but also taking a couple of steps between parallel bars. On top of that she could now lift her feet off the floor while sitting down and was also able to hold her pencil well enough to draw cubes. Mentally she was adept enough to count speedily back from one hundred to two in sevens. The children and I were simply dumbfounded by the pace of her progress.

Yet there was much more to come. By the following Monday Sue was walking the length of the whole huge ward with her Zimmer frame. She was also climbing up and down flights of stairs! She was able to dress herself. One of the team even suggested that she would soon be able to make a home visit in order to assess whether she was ready to return to her familiar surroundings. I wept for joy at the truly remarkable change that had come over her.

And just two days later she did indeed come home for a brief visit, with a physio on one arm and an occupational therapist on the other. She passed with flying colours the test of manoeuvring round our overcrowded home and even managed to climb the stairs, in spite of the fact they still had only one banister rail.

The date of this momentous visit was Wednesday 21st January, 2015. Less than three weeks earlier I had, with a very heavy heart, penned a letter to dear friends who themselves were seeking to come to terms with the terminal illness of their younger son, barely old enough for secondary school. The purpose of my letter was to report the distressing news that I had been told to find a nursing home for Sue, as the likelihood of either rehab or further treatment seemed very remote. That communication included these words: 'Sue also has many other discouragements to contend with, like today's realisation that she is largely incontinent as far as her bowel is concerned. Indeed, she is probably doubly incontinent as she has been catheterized since her operation six weeks ago. On top of that nausea is an almost permanent problem. Bless her, she is often cheerful, but facing dying is no easy thing.'

When he was told of the progress Sue was making, Alan Liu, who had been such a faithful friend at LGI, told me that he 'danced for joy, astonishment and praise to the Lord' at what he was hearing. And well he might. All the family felt like the author of Psalm 126: 'When the Lord restored our fortunes we were like those who dreamed.

Our mouths were filled with laughter, our tongues with songs of joy. The Lord has done great things for us, and we are filled with joy.'

A week later, on Friday 30th January, 2015, after a second banister rail had been fitted to the stairs and some other safety aids supplied for the bathroom, Sue came home to stay. It is a matter of profound thanksgiving that she never again needed to be an inpatient in hospital. Better still, for nearly the next two months, pretty well every day that followed her return saw evident improvement in her condition, whether measured by her mobility and dexterity, her energy levels, or her capacity to attempt new things.

Quite frankly it was just about the most wonderful time in our long marriage. We knew it might not last, though I did begin to wonder whether the Lord might not be healing Sue after all. But it was time together at home that we hadn't expected and progress we had not dared even to dream about.

Suddenly the most ordinary things seemed like very special treats. These included going out for a meal to a restaurant or friend's house, or even just sitting down to watch TV together. Astonishingly, pushing Sue round Dunelm Mill to buy new curtains for our bedroom, or even Sainsbury's for our weekly shop, provided immense pleasure. To me it was like being on our honeymoon all over again though, if I'm completely honest, much of my married life seemed like a honeymoon: and this was far more special.

Perhaps the highlight of those weeks was the occasion

that I drove Sue out to the National Trust property at Nostell Priory, east of Wakefield. It was a lovely afternoon, so on arrival I pushed Sue in the wheelchair from the main car park, through the rolling grounds almost to the main door of the striking stately home. Then we continued round the back of the property and down to the beautiful lake, where I helped Sue out of the wheelchair so that we could sit together on a bench and chat for a little while. It was wonderfully peaceful and Sue seemed blissfully happy.

After I had pushed her back up to the garden behind the house, Sue decided she wanted to get out and walk. I remember feeling very nervous about it, but I needn't have been. As I supported her arm, she walked easily at a sensible pace for more than two hundred yards before she got back into the wheelchair. At that point I remember kissing her head and squeezing her tight. Our hearts were singing. After all she had been through, and all that had been said to us, it seemed like we must be dreaming. Thankfully we weren't.

EIGHT

Brain frying and beyond

Radiotherapy and its disappointing outcome

JUST BEFORE SUE had finally come home from Bronte Tower I drove her to St James's Hospital (Jimmy's) in Leeds to talk with a couple of people in the Oncology Department about beginning treatment aimed at prolonging her life. They felt that she was still too weak to cope with chemotherapy but recommended a short course of radiotherapy as the best way forward. Sue would have just six sessions, administered at Jimmy's over a period of two weeks, rather than the normal thirty daily doses. However, her sessions would be greater in intensity, so that she would have more than half of the normal 'dose' in that brief time. The treatment was set to begin on Tuesday 24th February, just three and a half weeks after returning home.

While the oncology team's assessment of Sue's future prospects was still bleak, they sought to reassure us as to the likely value of the treatment and the limits of its unpleasant side-effects. They were confident that the radiotherapy would both prolong her life by delaying the growth of the tumour and improve the quality of the life that remained to her, at least for a while. They were also hopeful that Sue wouldn't find the treatment too difficult, believing that what side-effects it had wouldn't be too traumatic and wouldn't happen until after the travelling to and from Jimmy's was over.

Before the treatment commenced, Sue and I made a couple of other visits to Jimmy's for scans and the making of a plastic head mask. The latter was to enable them to keep her head completely still during the radiotherapy in order that the beams from the linear accelerator were accurately focussed. Sue took those visits in her stride and didn't appear fearful of the treatment that faced her. And when the treatment itself arrived she coped well with it, though she found having her head fixed in place for fifteen minutes at a time unpleasant.

Sadly, however, the optimistic noises about both the lack of side-effects from the treatment and its likely positive outcome proved unjustified. Headaches and nausea returned before the treatment was through, and intensified after it, when all Sue's hair came out, not just that growing around the three foci of the X-rays. She also began to feel much weaker and more lethargic, and never experienced the 'bounce' in her condition that she was almost promised would follow some weeks after the treatment. Worst of all, she was eventually told that the treatment had had absolutely no effect on the regrowth of the tumour.

Sue's returning symptoms never left her again. Steroids helped to control them and made life bearable. She also got used to some natty headgear after a brief trial with a glamorous wig never really worked out. And her new hand-knitted blankets served her well when she went out in the car or her wheelchair. She continued to have much joy in life, whether it was from being out in the park, drinking in the fresh air and marvelling at the lush new growth and the active squirrels, or chatting with the friends who came so often to see us.

At the beginning of April Sue suffered her first seizure — a pretty major one. It happened in the early hours of the morning while she was asleep. Because for many years we had looked after a delightful girl with epilepsy, it wasn't the first I had witnessed. What a kind providence it was that I had seen a seizure before and so was far less frightened than I would otherwise have been. However it was deeply distressing, and a severe reminder of just how poorly my beloved remained, notwithstanding the wonderful progress she had made since the beginning of the year.

After her convulsive shaking had stopped and I had put towels on the soaked bed, I rang our GP friend Deborah. Although it was three o'clock in the morning I urgently needed reassurance that I had handled the crisis aright and could safely let Sue sleep. Deborah patiently explained what had happened in layman's terms and sought to comfort me by saying that all would be well and that I could ring any time that I was anxious about Sue.

The seizure left Sue so tired that she didn't stir until mid-morning. When I took her to see her oncologist some days later we were warned that seizures could become a regular occurrence, even though medication would be given to lessen the likelihood of such an outcome. Therefore, I was grateful that, though Sue had a number of further fits in the remaining months of her life, they never became regular, nor was any other quite as severe as the first.

Within a few days of Sue's original diagnosis I had made the decision to send regular email updates on her health to family members and our many friends. The reasons for the decision were simple. First of all, many people were desperate to know how Sue was doing. This was a straightforward, time-saving way to keep in touch with a wide cross-section of people. And secondly, we felt out of our depth and were desperate that as many people as possible would help us by praying for us. We were keenly aware that we needed upholding by our gracious God if we were to honour him in this new and daunting phase of our lives.

Initially many of those updates were kindly written by our daughter-in-law Rachel, but I slowly began to realise that writing them myself was wonderfully therapeutic. They also gave me the opportunity to share with others some of our deepest thoughts about what was going on, and to explain the comforts that our Christian faith gave us even in the most stressful of moments. As a result, from the New Year I wrote all the updates myself. These sample extracts from letters written in April and May 2015 give an authentic insight into our struggles and comforts during this period of decline and disappointment.

Saturday 4ᵗʰ April. 'The Easter season is a great opportunity for us to express our joy and gratitude for the amazing love and thoughtfulness that has been showered upon us by so many over the last few difficult months. Time and again we have been encouraged and amazed by expressions and practical demonstrations of real affection from so many. And Easter is a time that gives hope in our sorrows, for the resurrection of Christ gives us grounded confidence that the death that is stalking us will not have the last word, and so can be faced with steadfastness and inner peace.'

Wednesday 15ᵗʰ April. 'You will be delighted to hear that last Tuesday, after Sue's hospital appointment, we did manage to get to our friends *(Frederick and Janet Hodgson)* in Sleights near Whitby. We had a wonderful time being looked after like royalty, and appreciating sweet companionship, lovely food, amazing weather, delightful views and being back by the sea. It did Sue a lot of good. We returned home on Friday, both very thankful for the break.

The hospital visit was a little disappointing. We were again well received and Sue was treated with care and compassion. But we were told not to count on any post-radiotherapy improvement in Sue's condition. We are expecting her to receive an appointment for another MRI scan soon which should show how far the tumour may have regrown.'

Sunday 3rd May. 'Dear friends. I am sorry it has been a while since I updated you on our situation. It is amazing how the days and weeks go by and how busy I seem to be — though, in truth, I get little done. Most days are spent doing the tasks necessary to look after the two of us and enjoying things together — like watching 'the News', 'Pointless' and 'Midsomer Murders'; playing 'Upwords' to stimulate both our brains; shopping together in the Supermarket; visiting friends and family, and enjoying their visits to us; and especially attending church on a Sunday morning.

Two things have disappointed me in the last month or so, but should not have been the surprise that they have. The first is to see Sue's strength and mobility deteriorate. We had hoped for some progress after the short course of radiotherapy but its debilitating effects seem to have outstripped any obvious benefits. Sue is finding movement and balance much more difficult, though she can still, at present, manage both the stairs and getting in and out of the car, as well as using her bath lift. However, increasing difficulties with all three make us wonder how long we will be able to carry on with the lifestyle into which we have happily settled.

The second disappointment has been my own tendency to impatience and crossness. It is easy to excuse it by citing my tiredness, caused both by many menial tasks and all the anxiety and distress I feel over Sue. Yet, in truth, it is as indefensible as it is reprehensible. It has only highlighted my need of God's mercy and transforming grace on an hourly basis. Sue deserves better from me, especially as she is so patient and appreciative of help given.

Well, that should give you a better picture of where we are at the moment, as well as furnishing you who kindly pray for us with ample materials to inform your intercession. Thank you all for your interest in, and love for, us both.'

Friday 8th May. 'I have been alarmed about how much Sue seems to have gone downhill just this past week, putting our much anticipated trip to Aberystwyth into jeopardy. She has a great deal of difficulty standing up anything like straight, and today, in spite of being in bed early last night, she is completely exhausted. She remains generally cheerful, though she is beginning to grasp just how poorly she is and how bleak the prospects of life in this world appear. Pray that her faith regarding the future world may flourish, even in her great weakness. God can do that for her and I am praying that he would. She continues to be a delight to look after, and appreciative of all that is done for her: bless her! Sorry to be the bearer of yet more depressing news.'

Sunday 17th May. 'I am delighted that Sue and I did manage our few days in Aberystwyth last week. Although Sue was weak, and largely spent the mornings in bed, we had a really lovely time, helped by excellent weather. We were royally looked after by our friends Gwyn and Glenys, whom we first met as students. Among the highlights were our trip up Constitution Hill on the cliff railway, an afternoon with old friends at Alfred Place Baptist Church, and a walk round the lake at the Red Kite Centre, up in the hills inland from Aber. We were both very grateful that we were able to return for a few delightful days to the place where we first met as undergrads.'

Wednesday 20th May. [*With reference to a key meeting with the oncologist*] 'We were apprehensive about what the specialist would tell us as Sue's health has declined considerably over the last month, both in terms of her general strength and her balance. Hence we were not really surprised when she gently told us that the latest MRI scan reveals considerable regrowth of her brain tumour which, disappointingly, the radiotherapy seems not to have arrested at all. She also confirmed that further treatment would be likely to make things more difficult for Sue without reaping any real benefits. We were glad that Matt and Beth [*our elder son and oldest daughter*] were able to be with us so that we could support each other in what was a difficult message for us to hear.

I continue to be surprised by the courageous and uncomplaining way that Sue copes with her severe weakness and the sobering news. She still shows a great sense of humour and a humbling tendency to be more concerned for me than for herself. Thankfully, in spite of spending much more time in bed, she is still able to summon up the strength both to go out with friends (especially if a coffee shop is involved) and to respond with joy to her visitors.

The coming weeks look very intimidating and I find myself wondering how either of us will cope. However, God's grace has proved more than sufficient so far, and we are confident, at least in our wiser moments, that it will prove just as effective in the surely difficult days that lie ahead. And we know that we will continue to have the support and help of our dear family and many proven friends. Indeed, whilst it will seem to many to be a very strange thing to say, life continues to provide us with many joys and even a sense of adventure, notwithstanding its heartaches. My bed calls. This comes with love from us both.'

NINE

Rapid decline

Sue becomes housebound, and time seems short

ALMOST AT THE end of May I sent this brief note to each of my five children. It highlights the kind of life issues that Sue was already facing, not all of which could be mentioned in the 'public' updates.

Beloved. Just to say Mum slept well all night (and dry), and ate a good breakfast. Since then I have successfully bathed her: better technique getting her in and out of the bath may extend that pleasure for Mum for a week or two more. She is now sleeping peacefully. Drowsiness and diminished inclination to chat are the main features of her gradual decline.

She will be up for lunch with Matt, Rachel and girls. Then she will stay up as we have Lucy and

Peter Beale visiting us mid-afternoon. Lucy was for many years the precious wife of my dear and esteemed friend, Alan Tovey, formerly of Beverley, now in glory. I miss him greatly. We first met him when he was travelling secretary to the IVF (now UCCF) in Wales when we were students. Mum likes Lucy and will be glad to see them both. They are gentle, godly folk.

Thanks for all your help, love, calls, visits and prayers.

Much love. Dad (and Mum!)

The arrival of June brought an increase in the pace of Sue's decline. It was so evident that I started to fear that she might not even last until the beginning of the school holidays. She had begun to feel an intense and debilitating weakness all the time she was out of bed. Her hours of sleep increased and she was rarely up for more than a couple of hours at a stretch. It was tough to watch her life ebbing away so quickly, however well she coped with her distressing condition and its pernicious symptoms. Yet in a strange way every extra day to lavish love and attention on her seemed like a real bonus.

Sue and I had made exciting plans to visit her beloved London for a weekend in early June. I had taken a booking to preach at the anniversary services of Hayes Town Chapel, where a friend of mine was the minister. Sue was particularly looking forward to it as we had planned to stay with Christine Tyler and her husband Garry in Harrow. Chris and Sue had been firm friends since causing much mischief together as teenagers at Dalston County Girls Grammar School in Inner East London, where Sue was brought up and from where she got her gorgeous Cockney accent. The two ladies had kept in touch for more than forty-five years, and we had enjoyed meeting up with Chris and Garry on quite a number of occasions in recent years, including one remarkable 'chance' meeting at a very out-of-the-way National Trust site in north Gloucestershire, far from either of our homes.

Sadly, when it came to the weekend, it was impossible for Sue to travel. It was just too much for her. However I went, chauffeured by Mike Howey, a long-standing friend. Meanwhile his wife, Chris, moved into our house for the weekend to look after Sue in my absence. Sue was very happy with the arrangements as she and Chris had been 'kindred spirits' and best buddies for decades.

In truth it was a really encouraging weekend for me, though I was somewhat anxious about Sue throughout my time away. I found a church deeply concerned about my situation, and very appreciative of the ministry I brought. My own heart was also stirred and strengthened as I showed others the wonderful tenderness of Christ to his followers, even when they are insensitive, self-absorbed and so slow to learn.

Best of all, I talked with quite a few people of different nationalities who had recently found life, joy and hope in the Lord Jesus. Such conversation inevitably boosts the spirit of any real believer (as in Acts 15:4). So whilst I missed Sue very much, as I always did when away overnight, and more so because I knew that she needed me more than ever, the break seemed to recharge my batteries as well as renewing my zeal and determination to love and care for her with all the skill, energy and tenderness that I could muster by God's grace.

The day before the London trip, a hospital bed was delivered to our home for Sue, which we put down stairs in our second, smaller living room. That was perfect timing for it meant that Sue no longer needed to go upstairs to bed, which made Christine's job in caring for her so much easier. Indeed, the only real worry I had felt in leaving my Sue with Chris had been about whether she would be able to manage her safely on the stairs. The exquisite timing of the provision of the bed was another indication of the Lord's detailed care for us, and as such it was a real spur to our faith. When I returned from London I took the decision that from that day forward I would sleep on cushions on the floor in what had become Sue's bedroom, which meant that I was able to be with her every night in case she needed me in the hours of darkness.

Later in June a stair lift was fitted in the house, enabling Sue to continue to go upstairs to bath and sometimes use the 'proper' toilet. Sadly, Sue's difficulty in getting onto both the lifts, for stairs and bath, meant that a fortnight or so later we had to make the decision that the rest of Sue's life would be lived downstairs.

By early July a hoist had arrived as it was impossible,

safely, to get Sue transferred from the bed to her portable commode. The commode was also narrow enough to serve as a wheelchair to get her into the living room. This meant that she could still spend the hours that she was up sitting in her favourite leather recliner, lent to us by our Chloe's in-laws, John and Liz Scott. They were among the very many who showed us great kindness during Sue's illness, kindness which continues towards me to this present day. Soon after this Sue's mobility deteriorated even further, requiring a second hoist for use in the living room and confining her to the home for the remaining months of her life.

Arguably the biggest change to our lives in July was the arrival of a care team from Social Services. They called four times a day to help me look after Sue. At first I was reluctant to accept their help, but I quickly found that their labours left me free to focus on Sue herself. It also gave our days a sensible structure.

Two ladies came first thing in the morning to wash or bed-bath Sue, get her dressed and even give her breakfast if I was stretched for time. It was a particular blessing to have help with dressing Sue as I had been struggling with that for a while, often taking an age to complete it. By this time Sue had become a fan of the reality TV programme 'Homes under the Hammer'. That meant she hadn't really minded how long it took her ham-fisted husband to get her ready for the day and looking smart for her visitors, though I think she sometimes found my struggles with buttons and clasps wearying.

Then one of the ladies would call again mid-morning to make sure Sue was comfortable and, perhaps, put her back in bed. A carer would return mid-afternoon, if necessary helping to get her up again. Finally, two would come between about seven and nine to put her to bed, or at least get her ready to go if she felt she wanted to sit up longer. Almost all the ladies were kind and gentle, as well as very efficient. They quickly became obviously fond of Sue, which was lovely for me to witness.

Initially this help was provided by a local authority team and I was distressed to realise that after six weeks it needed to change to a private company. Yet I need not have worried, for if anything those who came later were even more kind and helpful. Indeed, they had greater flexibility in terms of when they could come, and so managed to fit in better with our desires for the timing of both the morning and evening calls.

One surprising thing was that two of the youngest girls were the stars of a very good team. When I asked one of them one evening why they always took just a little more trouble with Sue (which involved working overtime for which neither of them were paid) she simply said, 'I like to treat all our clients as if they were my Gran.' Had it been appropriate I would have hugged her for that lovely spirit.

An email I sent on **July 10th 2015**, perfectly captures the flavour of our lives at that time:

Sue is still eating well and enjoying her food. Many friends have brought special meals which we have both loved. She is able to concentrate well enough to watch 'Miss Marple' or something similar on an evening, which is usually her best time. She loves seeing friends and family though she has little to say and often 'drops off'. She really appreciates it when visitors offer to read her a verse or two from the Bible and pray with her, and seems to be enjoying Mark's Gospel when we read a couple of paragraphs together each evening. I love to point out to her the incredible compassion of Jesus to those who come to him in distress and weakness.

Sometimes I find it overwhelmingly sad to see how weak she is and how little she can still do. Death is stalking her and its muddy footprints are everywhere. I well understand and share Dylan Thomas's rage against the 'dying of the light', against this unnatural and unwelcome guest we call death. Yet, thankfully, Sue knows that Christ has triumphed over death, not just for Himself but for all who both hope in him and come to God through him. My greatest concern for her is that she might increasingly know the comfort of that truth as she faces the difficult business of dying.

One of the most distressing aspects of Sue's illness at

this time was the way it began to steal from her not only her mobility but also her speech. All her adult life she had been a most adept conversationalist, all delivered in authentic East End Cockney with an impressive grasp of English grammar and an extraordinarily wide vocabulary, the latter gained and maintained by omnivorous reading. Many was the time during our marriage when I'd ask her to explain a word she had just used. Almost invariably she looked startled at my ignorance, but could always provide a dictionary-perfect definition for the words she used so naturally. I use a dictionary much more now that my personal one is in heaven! Yet now she was beginning to find speech more difficult. It mostly seemed just a problem with engaging her brain. As a result, often even a simple question of what she wanted to drink seemed beyond her, even when it was presented as a choice of just two alternatives. Yet all the while she appeared to remain largely at peace and grateful for all that was done for her.

TEN

A changed lady?

'How was Sue different after the tumour struck?'

FRIENDS ASKED me a number of times in Sue's last months what was different about her post-operatively from the woman I had lived with all those years. I guess the question may have been prompted by the very obvious change in her appearance. The brutal truth was that within about seven months of the operation the vile thing that was spreading in her brain, aided by the stress she had faced and the medication she was taking, had changed her from a strikingly attractive lady who looked years younger than her true age to a very overweight, frankly elderly, woman. Indeed, one person who was shocked to see the change in her did ask me, perhaps almost involuntarily, how I was coping with the sad transformation.

I still find that a difficult question to answer. I was certainly very conscious of the cruel change in her appearance. It was sad to see how quickly a lady who had made considerable efforts to keep herself looking nice for her doting husband had been marred by a horrible disease. We all know that physical beauty cannot last for ever in this fallen and cursed world. Yet to see the ageing clock run at the shockingly rapid pace that it did with Sue was disturbing. Indeed, so significant was the change in her appearance that some who knew her quite well admitted that they had needed to look three times at the lady I was pushing in the wheelchair to realise that it was Sue. It brought home to me how serious was Adam's rebellion that it could bring this kind of affliction on his descendants.

Perhaps my feelings about her, now the disease had so marred her, can best be judged from some words I wrote to a kind and sympathetic friend at the end of August, 2015: 'Dear Norman, thanks for your kind words. My dear Sue looks so much older and steroid-bloated than twelve months ago, but still has a beautiful smile.' Incidentally, that trademark smile led later visitors to remark that her face looked like 'the face of an angel', a compliment famously paid to the evangelist Stephen in the New Testament.

My letter to Norman continued: 'Indeed, in a strange way her smile is more beautiful still, coming from the heart of someone whose life is so blighted. I love her more than ever and am immensely proud of her. Grace makes people beautiful and delightful. What a wonderful place glory will be, just to see all the perfected trophies of God's inimitable grace, let alone to see the God of all grace Himself!'

Yet alterations to her appearance were not the only striking differences we saw in Sue. And some of the other changes were positive and brought me real joy. They gave me significant reasons to thank my God, and even served to strengthen my long-held, but under-pressure, faith — in spite of all the pain that Sue's illness was causing me. What were those changes?

Well, Sue had always been a person who was prone to **anxiety** about what might happen in the future to her or those she loved. On a number of occasions our elder son, Matthew, was astonished by his mum's ability to imagine potential disasters that might befall one of her children or grandchildren. Yet throughout her struggles that followed the arrival of the tumour she seemed far less anxious than in her previous healthy life, and sometimes even relaxed about what had befallen her.

Doubtless a significant part of the reason for that change was the fact that the brutal operation had removed so much material from the front of her brain. Apparently this tends to make people less inhibited, and so perhaps less anxious. Yet that never seemed a sufficient explanation for the strikingly positive change I and others saw in Sue.

The question I pondered was this: how could this woman, who was always fearful that one of us would become so ill as to rob us of our retirement bliss, be so placid and uncomplaining in the face of all that had happened? It wasn't as if she had ceased to be affectionate, or stopped caring deeply about her family. No, that wasn't the change. What I now saw in her was that in the face of terrible suffering, and with the distress of losing a future that she had looked forward to with joy and expectancy, she was far less inclined to be anxious than hitherto. More than that, not only did she seem not really anxious about what faced her but she never showed, let alone expressed, anger at what was happening to her. And more remarkably still, I never detected frustration at the disappearance of her long-cherished dream of a more relaxed life with lots of time for each other.

Significantly, this change was not immediately apparent after the operation. Indeed, while she was in LGI she often talked with determination that we must press on quickly with our previously agreed plan to move house. I found that very disconcerting. It seemed to show that she wasn't facing the reality that she was terminally ill, nor the truth that even if she did make sufficient progress to come home she would never be able to face the trauma of moving. Yet I need not have worried, for when she did manage to come home she always seemed strangely content with her lot and fully resigned to the reality that she would soon be leaving this world.

So momentous was the change in her that it was impossible for me not to link it with the fact that literally hundreds of people were praying daily for her. And certainly that contentedly calm spirit made the task of looking after her so much easier than if she had been constantly wracked by anxiety.

Closely allied to that change was another marked transformation in her mood and outlook, for in the last nine months of her life Sue appeared totally free of the **depression** that had been a feature of her life during the second half of our marriage. Even many who knew her well will be surprised to know that Sue ever suffered with depression, not least because she was famous for her warm smile and happy laugh. She generally managed to hide her depression from most people, helped by the fact that it was never persistent. It would rarely last more than a week or two and then would return after perhaps two or three months. Nor was it bad enough to need medication. Yet it was very real, and distressing for us both.

Sometimes it seemed to have a particular cause and be related to her anxiety problem, as when our daughter Beth and her husband Sergey were about to take the children to Kazakhstan for a mid-winter visit. At other times it just seemed to be 'the blues' and utterly inexplicable. Yet at times it was bad enough for me to try to have fewer evenings out or to forgo attending a ministers' conference. However, I never admitted to Sue that she was the reason for changes in the routine of a man whose life was generally so predictable!

I suppose that the changes that struck me most about Sue in her illness were not great alterations in her character or habits, but rather the final and most beautiful flowering of graces, wrought by the Spirit of God, which I and many others had long admired in her. There was her *patience* as day after day her condition (and other people) dictated the pattern of her life, and carers or visitors could not always come at the times they promised. There was also her *uncomplaining spirit*, and deep and warmly expressed gratitude for pretty well every service done for her, even when it was simply part of a person's job. On top of that her *courage* in the face of all she was suffering was unwavering and inspiring.

One particular joy was her ability to see the funny side of even seemingly tragic reminders of her failing strength. Typical was the day when I tried to emulate her carers and transfer her from the recliner to the small wheeled commode, only to allow her to slide helplessly to the floor. I was so embarrassed at my failure, and troubled lest it meant that I would have to call out the emergency ambulance to get her up again. Sue's reaction was to grin at me and chuckle about her predicament. Thankfully, in the end I managed to get a number of church people round to lift her up without damage to Sue or themselves. Yet it brought home to me that I had never met anyone so *inclined to laugh at herself*. I also noticed that in the last few months of her life Sue's tendency to chuckle in situations that would have led most people to weep or complain was a real tonic to those who witnessed it.

Yet it was the consistency and depth of *her love for me*, her affectionate but unobservant (and frankly rather inept) husband, that really shone out to me in the closing months of her life. In truth it often brought me to tears of joy, astonishment or intense grief. Whether it was the day she was told she had only a few months to live, or the time that the doctor asked her about end of life care and resuscitation, or when I falteringly broached the subject of where she preferred to die, it was her preoccupation with what was best for me that both made me feel like the most loved man in the world and broke my heart. What would persuade anyone to make such personal decisions as to whether to leave home for hospital, or whether to endure a crash team when they got there, simply by what would be easiest for their spouse? But that was Sue's rationale, and to me it was breathtakingly beautiful.

Sure, Sue was a long way from being a perfect woman. Like most of us, she could at times be very stubborn, and didn't find it easy to admit when she was in the wrong. She could also be quite controlling, and was sometimes peeved when family members couldn't be persuaded to fit in with her plans. On occasions her daughters experienced rather harsh and frankly unkind words. And at times she could even get impatient with her beloved grandchildren. More seriously, she often struggled really to believe what the Bible told her of God's love for her and all he was promising to do for her. Yet all the things that I have outlined in this chapter were true of her, and showed me that Sue was growing more like her Saviour and more fitted for heaven on a daily basis.

However, she would never have recognised or countenanced that description of herself. And though it may seem strange to many of my readers to say it, I need to add that of all the things I observed in Sue in the last year of her life, that which gives me most joy, gratitude and assurance is that she seemed to know very clearly that she was in as great a need of the efficacy of the Saviour's death for sinners then as in the day she first sought it as a student, after being convicted of her sin under the preaching of Dr Martyn Lloyd-Jones. In that alone lies my confidence that she is now in the presence of God where her joy is unimaginable, awaiting the day when her body will also be raised in glory at the return of Christ.

ELEVEN

Sue's Indian summer

Two months of unexpected stability

THERE WERE days in mid-July 2015 when it seemed as if the end could be as little as a fortnight away. So quickly was Sue fading, and so overwhelmingly tired did she seem, that I just couldn't see how she could live much beyond the end of the month. She had begun to have issues with breathlessness on top of all her other distressing symptoms, and one generally helpful on-line site indicated that the cluster of symptoms that she showed might well mean that she had less than two weeks left to live. The children and I braced ourselves for what seemed the inevitable.

However, surprisingly and wonderfully, as the end of July approached Sue's health began to improve somewhat. Better still, from then on she experienced more than two months in which her condition hardly changed — a kind of blessed Indian summer for us all to catch our breath, and to say a much more leisurely 'farewell' to a beloved friend. It was an extraordinary mercy from our loving heavenly Father. It also gave me the time to see more clearly than ever what a remarkable lady, of rare inner beauty, grace had made my precious Susie, and just how blessed I had been all those years to be her husband.

Sure, life was still very limited for a woman who was used to working extremely hard and cramming her time with all manner of things — mostly service to others. She was still shut-in and spending most of the day in bed, and within a very few weeks she would be effectively mute. Yet her breathing improved again and she seemed much more alert than before. Most pleasing of all in terms of her health, she continued to have almost no pain, in spite of all that was going on with the tumour and the fact that she generally spent between eighteen and twenty hours a day in bed.

Yet the next more than two months were a very special time for the two of us, and Sue thoroughly enjoyed what life she had. She relished seeing the children and grandchildren, welcoming friends from near and far, and excitedly looking at cards and post cards which arrived from the four corners of Britain and far beyond. Having been read, those cards all took their place on the doors and walls of the living room nearest to Sue's comfortable recliner. And, to my great delight, simple pleasures like watching TV, eating her dinners, or even enjoying a McDonald's breakfast, often brought a wide and lasting smile to her face. However, those months seemed to pass very quickly and I find it disconcerting that my memory of them is rather hazy.

Part of the reason for this is that little happened beyond what was by now our well-established, normal routine. The nurses arrived soon after seven every morning and gently washed Sue and made her more comfortable. Then we had breakfast together and she snoozed until mid-morning, at which time the carers came again. This visit was to change her incontinence pad, and it provided the opportunity for us to share a drink and biscuit together, as well as to read some verses from Scripture. During this period of her life we mostly read everything we could find in the Bible about the blessings that await the believer in the future, both immediately after death and when the Saviour returns in glory.

Lunch was about one, and then Sue would sleep further until the carers returned around four to hoist her out of bed and transfer her to the living room. Generally she was at her most awake then and we would watch TV or a DVD together, or entertain the many visitors who kindly came to see us. The arrival of visitors also gave me opportunity to spend a little time sorting out what we were having for our main meal of the day.

To the very end Sue loved to see her visitors. Among the highlights for us both were visits from two couples living overseas who went to considerable lengths to be able to fit us in to their busy holiday schedules in the UK. They were Andrew and Daphne Swanson from Turkish Cyprus, and Irfon and Ann Hughes from the USA. Both Andrew and

Irfon became valued ministerial colleagues of mine when I first moved to Dewsbury, and Sue was thrilled to see Daphne and Ann again, women whom she greatly admired and whose wisdom, friendship and prayerful support had meant a great deal to her over so many years.

Having spoken of Sue's joy at seeing old friends from afar, I need also to report that her regular, more local visitors also contributed so much to keeping Sue's spirits up over the months when she was shut-in and starting to lose the power of speech. Of no one was this more true than Angela Donnelly. Sue and Angela had become firm friends over the years when Angela was passing through deep waters, and now that Sue was in great need Angela became a real strength to her. No one who came appreciated like Angela that Sue's need was to have someone there who was happy to chat, but didn't feel uncomfortable with long periods of silence when Sue felt weary.

As autumn arrived I was spending almost all my time in the home. To achieve this I learned to order our shopping on-line, even though it often took me longer to do it than if I had gone round the supermarket! I often discussed with Sue what she would like from the shop in order to involve her as much as possible in the running of the home. Generally I then had the order delivered at a time when I knew Sue would be asleep, so that I could give her my full attention when she was awake.

Yet I was not entirely housebound. I did get to Dewsbury Evangelical Church most Sunday mornings, thanks to the kindness of a number of ladies from the fellowship who came to look after Sue while I was there. I treasured the times of being fed from God's word, and sought to share what had blessed my soul with Sue when I returned home. It was also lovely to be among God's people again, and sometimes overwhelming to be the object of such concern and sympathy. Yet I greatly missed being involved in the day-to-day life of the church, though I would never have swapped the more personal pastoral work that providence had given me in caring for Sue.

I also had a few hours out one day almost every week to relax, while Chris Howey came to look after Sue. I generally took a drive somewhere, parked and went for a stroll into a lonely place to muse, pray or read a book. At other times I simply found somewhere full of life to watch the world, or sometimes the trains, go by. One very special day I went to Marsden to have lunch and walk by the canal with Steve Saxton, a friend I had known even longer than I had known Sue; but always after just a few hours I was eager to return to look after my best friend.

Domesticity came hard, though the service was gladly rendered to the lady whose speed and efficiency in household duties were legendary and the envy of many. Indeed, I felt it was a great honour to care for her. Yet I was also glad and grateful for all the help I received with that work, including cleaning (generally done by our daughter-in-law Rachel) and the preparation of a whole array of delightful meals (done mostly, but not exclusively, by the ladies of Dewsbury Evangelical Church).

Towards the end of September I wrote to many friends

about our situation, and particularly the blessing that our children were proving to both Sue and myself. The email was headed, 'The Joy of an Indian Summer' and really sums up life at the time:

For me, and I believe the same is true to some degree even for Sue, the last few months have been like an Indian summer — a delightful time, and all the more joyful for being unexpected. To be sure it has been distressing just watching on helpless as Sue has become gradually bedridden, functionally incontinent and unable to do hardly anything for herself. Yet, having been told shortly after Christmas that she was unlikely ever to be well enough to come home, all we have enjoyed together has been a huge bonus.

And still, in spite of the fact that she has had a couple of distressing fits in the last eight days, there is so much pleasure in simply being together and…. seeing the kindness of so many friends. We are blessed indeed! One thing that has really made a difference is the love of our children and their life partners.

Matt and Rachel live round the corner and are always helping, with meals, visits and many acts of thoughtful love. Phil has often made the trek from Yate, in spite of far from good health. Indeed, he and Ruth are on their way as I write, and bringing food for us to enjoy together, even though Ruth is stretched with the children, as well as anxieties over her own parents.

Our girls and their soulmates have also been marvellous. Beth loves to visit her Mum, often bringing her three to visit Grandma. And her husband Sergey delights to come with homemade pancakes, pasties or pelmeni (tasty Russian food, not unlike ravioli). Jo is here every weekend, combining working nights locally with supporting her mum, and supplying cakes and other edible delights, while her husband Michael looks after their boys. She rings every day to make sure we are coping and constantly bemoans how little she does for us. And our Chloe and her Kyle bring their two little ones every other weekend from Chelmsford, and Chloe gently runs the household while she is here, giving her tired old Dad a lovely rest.

So you see, while life is very hard for my beloved, it is also heavily laced with things that bring deep joy. And no joy is deeper for me than to see the peace and patience that daily mark her, the fruit of God's daily grace in Christ and a token of the future that awaits her.

By the end of September it was apparent that her 'Indian summer' was almost over, and that the sands in her life-glass were fast running out. Accordingly, on October 1st I sent the following note to our many faithful friends, under the heading, 'The Home Straight?'.

As I write this I am painfully aware that since I last wrote [September 22nd 2015] there has been a marked decline in Sue's health and strength. Last Sunday she had a further minor seizure and since then she has been noticeably more tired. She no longer 'gets up' routinely each afternoon, nor does she always wake up when the ladies come to check and change her each morning. And she looks more poorly and struggles even more to answer the simplest question. Accordingly I have abandoned my proposed trip to Maryport this coming weekend [where I was booked to preach], and am thankful that it was an easy decision in the end, made easier still by the graciousness of the folks I was going to serve.

All this has made me, and others, wonder whether Sue's life in this world is drawing towards a close — hence the strap-line to this update. In truth, of course, we don't know what time she has left, whether days, weeks, or even months. Only the Sovereign Lord of all knows that. But the signs are that she has almost 'run her course'. However, she still has her evident joys, which this week have included the arrival of beautiful flowers, visits from friends with their four month old son, enjoying a delightful 'chicken in creamy mushroom sauce' cooked for us by someone in our church, and watching with me the BBC adaptation of 'Cider with Rosie' and some World Cup rugby — Sue's choice, I kid you not!

It remains a great joy for me to look after her. I believe that I am at last learning the wisdom, and indeed the life-transforming simplicity, of living a day at a time. I can only attribute it all to the astonishing grace of God towards me in Christ. Once more I close with warm thanks for your love for us and interest in our welfare and small doings.

TWELVE

Falling asleep in Jesus

The end of Sue's life on earth

WHEN THE END of Sue's earthly pilgrimage did eventually come it was surprisingly less traumatic, strung out or bleak than I had feared. Indeed, strange as it will probably sound, most of my memories of Sue's last days are positive and even beautiful.

Thursday October 22nd, the last day on which Sue was to eat a meal, was my birthday. It was sixty-six years before that I first saw the light of day in a hospital just a few hundred yards east of the Vicarage Road ground of my beloved Watford FC. Sue had been in bed all day, but in the early evening our son-in-law, Sergey, had come to visit, bringing with him a Russian meal for us to enjoy. The meal was a favourite of Sue's, but almost for the first time since her illness struck she had very little appetite. I slowly fed her just a little of the meal so that she could keep her strength up, but she really found it difficult and the effort exhausted her.

Though her appetite had generally been good throughout her trial, Sue had experienced considerable struggles with drinking for a few weeks now. Her problem seemed to be an increasing difficulty in controlling her throat muscles. I had been advised by a friend who is a speech therapist that Sue would cope more easily with thicker liquids, like soups or smoothies, rather than with her favourite beverage, tea — and so it had proved. Yet, with the exception of one or two lunchtimes, eating had generally given Sue pleasure until that evening.

In spite of trying for Sergey's sake, Sue could manage no more food or drink and she settled down to sleep while Sergey and I talked a little before he returned home. Eventually I once more put my cushions on the floor in the room that had become Sue's whole world and slept well, having first committed us both to the care of our heavenly Father.

The next morning was very traumatic. After the carers had been to wash Sue and make her comfortable, her breathing suddenly became erratic and she was soon gasping desperately for air. I called the emergency line for the district nurses and was told a senior lady was on her way to medicate Sue. To my great relief, while I waited for her to arrive, Chris Howey, herself a nurse, arrived and together we tried to comfort Sue.

I can vividly remember those endless minutes of waiting. It was heart breaking to witness my sweetheart's struggle, and to hear Chris whisper in my ear that she hoped the nurse would arrive soon as she feared the frantic effort to catch her breath would take Sue to her eternal home. In the event that didn't happen. Two nurses arrived, followed by Sue's GP, Dr Spencer. Then, in response to the administration of suitable medication, Sue's breathing became far less laboured, and she was fast asleep again. It proved to be a sleep from which she never truly awoke.

Talking of sleep, that Friday night was the first time in many months that I had slept upstairs in our house in a proper bed. Following the traumas of that morning the district nurses had kindly arranged for a Marie Curie nurse to come to the house mid-evening in order to sit with Sue all night. It was a strange experience to vacate the floor next to Sue's amazing hospital bed and trudge 'up the wooden hill' to sink again into a proper mattress. But sleep I did, and the rest did me a lot of good. The same was destined to happen on the next two nights also, but the second of those would be interrupted to witness the Lord take my Susie home. But I run ahead of myself.

The next day, Saturday October 24th, was notable for two events to which Sue and I had both been long looking forward. Around mid-day we had visitors to our home all the way from Cornwall. Nick and Sarah Fuller were in the area for a wedding, and had kindly promised to call. Nick had been the second pastor at Mirfield Evangelical Church, a fellowship which had been planted with my help largely by members from Dewsbury in the mid-1980s. They had left for new work in Truro around the time when Sue was transferred to rehab in Dewsbury District Hospital. Sarah and Sue had been close friends for the eight years the Fullers had spent in West Yorkshire. Unfortunately, Sue was largely asleep while Nick, Sarah and their daughter Abigail were with us, but it was a joy for me to see them and they were pleased that Sue had lived long enough for them to say goodbye to her personally.

That same evening at Central Offices, the new home of Dewsbury Evangelical Church, a party had been arranged to mark the 70th birthdays of our dear friends Colin and Judith Mountain. Colin was a founder member of the church, and theirs was the first wedding I ever conducted, back in March 1978. Sadly, with Sue so poorly neither of us could attend the celebrations: in truth, I felt very uncomfortable that our troubles would inevitably dampen those proceedings at least somewhat.

That weekend our youngest daughter Chloe arrived as planned to see her mum, leaving her children with her in-laws. Her presence was another sweet providence from the Lord, for it meant that I could sit with Sue for long periods without needing to busy myself with food preparation, household chores, or answering the inevitable stream of kindly phone calls. Remembering again those wonderful 'coincidences', woven into our lives by the God who works all things together for the good of those who love him, is one of the great joys and benefits of writing a memoir like this.

Sunday passed without significant incident or apparent change, and I began to be anxious about how many days it might be before the Lord eventually took Sue to himself. I remember praying very earnestly that he would do it speedily — surely one of the strangest prayers I have ever prayed. I was asking fervently and wholeheartedly for the thing I most dreaded in life.

That prayer was gently and lovingly answered in the early hours of Monday morning, October 26th 2015. I was deeply asleep upstairs around three o'clock when there was a gentle knocking on my bedroom door. I woke understanding what was happening, something that isn't always the case with me! The motherly Marie Curie nurse advised me that Sue had begun to show signs that the end might be fairly near, and recommended that I get fully dressed and came down to sit with her. As I put on the clothes I had laid out the evening before, I felt surprisingly calm, and was glad to be able to pray for grace for us both in what lay ahead. I also wondered what might face me when I came to Sue.

However, when I saw Sue I was surprised to be able to detect no change whatever from how I had left her when I went to bed. Indeed, to my untrained ear she was breathing normally and appeared to be sleeping very peacefully. I remember wondering what the nurse had seen to awaken in her the conviction that the end was near. And yet the passing of less than half an hour would prove that she was absolutely right. Doubtless it was a kind of intuition born of sitting at the bedside of many dying patients.

Fairly soon after this our night sitter asked me if there was anyone nearby who would appreciate the opportunity to be with Sue when she died. I thought it might well be too painful an experience for soft-hearted Chloe, but rang Matthew who lives less than half a mile away. While I waited for Matt to arrive I held and stroked his mother's soft, warm hand.

Less than five minutes later, the nurse said she would leave me alone with Sue for a little while and within ninety seconds, before Matt had time to arrive, Sue breathed for the final time. It struck me then that it was the last breath she would breathe until the voice of the returning Saviour would call her dust from the grave on that great resurrection morning for which the church has looked for so long.

I am tremendously grateful that Sue's was a beautifully peaceful passing. Her gentle breathing just stopped. There was no last racking gasp for air, nor the stop-start ending that marks so many deaths. I was simply left squeezing and kissing that soft, warm hand and looking lovingly into that unnaturally aged face that had so often returned my adoring gaze with a beautiful smile. Susie had gone where I cannot follow until my Lord and Master decrees that my life's work here is done. I had lost my dearest friend and only lover — and yet felt so thankful for her, and oh so proud of her.

The rest of that night is a blur in my mind. Matthew arrived and we talked, mostly about his mum. We called Chloe down and wept together, and talked some more. Together we praised the Lord for all that Sue had been to us. We also blessed him for the cast-iron hope we have for the future, including being reunited with the one we had just lost, a hope based on the most stubborn fact of history, namely Jesus' bodily resurrection on the third day after his savage judicial execution.

Later the district nurses and the undertaker's assistants arrived, and Sue's precious body was duly removed from the place that had been her home for more than thirty years. Finally the angel of a nurse also left, without fuss or formality, having performed a wonderfully tender yet professional service for those who had been complete strangers just a few hours before.

Some days later I went to see Sue's body at the chapel of rest with our Beth, who 'wanted to see her mum.' But we didn't see her. What we saw was her lifeless body, albeit very precious to us and to her Lord. She had been carefully dressed in characteristic blouse and skirt, all beautifully ironed, and a little make-up had been tastefully applied to her swollen face. Yet that body was lifeless and empty, a stark reminder of the brutal reality of death.

However, not all was gloom and pain in the days following Sue's death, for at that time I received a veritable avalanche of beautiful cards expressing deep sympathy with me and the children in our loss. And many of those cards contained wonderful tributes to Sue which only served to underline the privilege that had been mine to have such a lady as my wife for more than forty-three years. Typical of those notes were these beautiful testimonies.

I am so thankful for Sue and her lovely life, and for all the blessings she brought to the lives of your family, the church, and the wider Christian community . . . Sue had such an attractive personality: genuinely interested in other people, down to earth and yet with an inner radiance that drew others to her. The way in which she faced her illnesses and heartaches is a wonderful testimony to the grace of God in her life. She was a beautiful person inside and out.

We thank the Lord for Sue's laughter. We can still hear her laugh, and thank the Lord that in her living out of Proverbs 31 she has given us an example to follow in both our marriage and our ministry.

Like many others I have happy memories of her lovely smile and sense of fun, and her generous and kind spirit that reached out to people.

Sue was such a lovely soul, a treasure, and so wonderfully human — the hallmark of a mature Christian. It was impossible not to be drawn to her by the warmth and spontaneity of her personality combined with her transparent godliness. I count it one of the great privileges of my life to have known her. She will always be affectionately remembered.

Those cards not only helped to sustain me in the immediate aftermath of Sue's death but often since then. They brought home to me more fully than ever two truths that I had been sinfully slow to grasp. The first was that many others felt *for themselves* something of my profound sense of loss in the death of my dear Sue. The other was that the Lord has blessed me with an amazing number of caring and faithful friends accumulated through my rich and varied life, from the cradle to retirement.

THIRTEEN

Dust to dust

The day of Sue's funeral

SUE'S funeral was planned for Friday, November 6th 2015, some eleven days after her death — the delay was to make it easier for those who wanted to attend to arrange time off work, sort travel plans, find provision for the care of children, and in some cases even book overnight accommodation. We expected a large crowd of mourners, for Sue was a well-known and much loved lady. And we were right in that judgement.

I woke long before dawn on that fateful morning, feeling very intimidated by all that lay ahead of me. So, as has long been my habit, I turned to the Bible for comfort and reassurance, and found these words written by Paul the apostle that pretty well mirrored my own emotional state and also that of my dear children: 'We are hard pressed on every side, but not crushed; perplexed, but not in despair; struck down, but not destroyed' (2 Corinthians 4:8-9). I took heart from Paul's assertion that what positivity I did have was God's doing, not mine (see 4:7).

Reading on in that passage I found the very things I needed more than anything else, if I was not to be crushed by the realisation of what death had snatched from me. Firstly, I found words to pray, namely that God would strengthen me and my family as he had Paul and his friends, so that we too would be able to declare honestly, 'We do not lose heart' (4:1). I also dared to pray that God would help me so to see the glory that awaits those who trust in His Son that I could even view losing Sue as a 'light and momentary affliction' compared to what is promised me (4:17).

Yet I found so much more than urgently needed fuel for prayer. I found solid reasons for being confident that death and the cruel grave were not the last word that could be said for Sue. Paul reminded me that because of Christ's triumph over death for her, Sue was even now 'with the Lord' (5:8). Better still, I read of a day when 'mortality would be swallowed up with life' (5:4). Strengthened by what I read, I resolved to fill my mind that day with those things about which I had read, which though 'unseen' are gloriously true and immensely encouraging.

I had arranged that before the children and I would face the ordeal of the graveside, we would lunch together on shop-bought fish and chips at our church building with all the extended family who could be present. It proved a good move, a gentle and mutually supportive preparation for what lay ahead. Sue's nieces, Wendy and Fiona, were there with Wendy's husband Clive. They had driven up from north Devon, scene of many of our family's happiest holidays, to be with us. Her remaining sister, Judy, joined us later, with her husband Eamonn and their daughter Lucy. My two brothers were there, and my sister-in-law, and my five children and their spouses. It was a bitter-sweet gathering, but a precious one nevertheless.

Arriving at the strikingly rural Liversedge cemetery, I felt very alone even though a hundred or so mourners were there with me, almost all of whom were dear personal friends. What struck me was that most of them were in couples, and that the ones who had most reasons to grieve at Sue's passing were holding tight to their spouses. It was a poignant reminder of what I had lost. And yet even there I saw the Lord's thoughtfulness towards me as my eyes lighted on one dear friend who needed my arm.

Sue and I had known Dawn since we were students in Aber. Indeed Sue had lived with her family through most of our courtship. Then a lovely providence had brought her to teach locally, and she settled in Dewsbury, married here and was blessed (like us) with five children. Now she has MS and, as her husband wasn't able to get off work until the second service, there was Dawn needing support to walk across the graveyard. Dawn was my distraction, and a lovely reminder that I could find real wholeness and peace in life without Sue if I focussed on serving and supporting others.

Another great source of strength at the cemetery was

the fact that I had known the undertakers for decades, during which time we had worked together on many funerals. That contact bred deep mutual respect that has blossomed into real friendship. Neil, Helen and Judith are the children of the late George Brooke, who started the family funeral business some years before Sue and I moved to Dewsbury. His children share their father's kindly, down-to-earth, and servant-hearted approach to their important work, and as a result their business is very well respected in the town. Rain was threatening as I arrived at the cemetery and it was a reassurance to know that the Brookes would have everything in hand. And so it proved as we stood under three giant gazebos for protection from a few spots of rain. What I hadn't anticipated, but greatly appreciated, was that all three would be present at some time that afternoon to show their support for me and regard for Sue.

I found the sight of the grave very intimidating. There before me was a deep chasm into which we would be lowering a box holding the earthly remains of a woman who had shown such vitality in life. What a vile, cruel enemy this death is, that it devastates us so completely. However, I knew that we weren't there to admit defeat by expressing a cowering submission to death. We were there to repudiate, challenge and even pour scorn on it. That we did in two acts of defiance: preaching a gospel of hope that offers eternal life and the bodily resurrection of the dead, and singing a rousing hymn of praise to Jesus the Christ who himself conquered death.

It was highly appropriate that the preacher was Mick Lockwood, then pastor of Hall Green Baptist Church in Haworth. Mick and I had become great buddies as young men when he was serving the Baptist church in Thornhill, a suburb of Dewsbury. There he had preached and lived out the message that had completely revolutionised his life when a teenager from a rough estate who had dabbled in drugs. Hearing him preach so soberly and yet confidently at the graveside reminded me of a Sunday decades before when I stood in for him at Thornhill as his own dear wife, Gill, was stricken down with a brain haemorrhage. Thankfully Gill survived and has been his great helpmeet ever since.

The first line of the hymn we sang by that open grave was 'Thine be the glory, risen conquering Son, endless is the victory, thou o'er death has won.' It was sung with faith and great gusto by almost all of those who were present. And I knew deep down that one day the power of God will show the reality and true scale of Christ's triumph, and prove how superficial and temporary is the victory death has gained over my Sue.

The service in the cemetery was followed by one at Central Offices, the home of Dewsbury Evangelical Church. It was conducted by my good friend and successor there, Daniel Grimwade, and was full of rich encouragement for me in my hour of need. Over two hundred and fifty people gathered there to share our sorrow and support us in our grief. The undying God was worshipped with reverence and passion, and his word was preached with faithfulness and clarity. Friends came from far and wide to honour Sue and thank God for his grace in her life. It was moving, delightful and in every way encouraging to my soul, not least because it recognised the place for grief and sorrow whilst at the same time reinforcing godly Christian hope.

Sue was portrayed before us in striking word pictures. First, I was enabled briefly to explain how I had lost my heart to her when we were students in mid-Wales. Then our Matt spoke movingly, yet with appropriate humour, about his dear mum. Finally Chris Howey vividly illustrated the qualities of one of her very best friends.

Those word pictures were reinforced both before and after the formal service by the projection of a series of photos of Sue spanning her whole life. They revealed a lady who spent so much of her life smiling at others, and who was delightedly devoted to the service of her husband, five children, thirteen grandchildren, and literally scores of friends. Finally, it was lovely that the many who stayed behind to talk to me and all the family about the beautiful lady who had so graced all our lives were shown the wonderful hospitality of the church that had supported us both through every moment of the toughest year of our lives.

And so a momentous day that started for me with apprehension, earnest prayer and soul-strengthening Bible study ended with deep gratitude and real spiritual certainty. God had truly heard my cries. Yet I was now alone, though determined to go on joyfully wearing the ring that Sue had given me on our wedding day. Our one-flesh union was over, never to be restored. And yet I knew I was not alone, nor ever would be.

It wasn't just that I knew I was blessed with deeply affectionate children and grandchildren, and a whole array of kind and caring friends. The day had so clearly demonstrated that. My confidence regarding the future in this world was bolstered by something better still. I knew that the Lord who had brought Sue to me, had blessed us in all our happy years of marriage, and had walked with us in the valley of deep shadow, would never leave me or forsake me. And I knew, too, that my parting from Sue would be only for a few short years at the most, until I too enter into the joy that is now hers. Furthermore, I also knew that, until that day comes, I can reflect with great thankfulness on the happiest of lives, shared with a lady who so faithfully kept every one of her sacred marriage vows. For that inestimable blessing I can, must and do praise my Lord every day.

FOURTEEN

Learning a new life

Adapting to life as a widower

IT IS no exaggeration for me to say that Sue's home-call started me on a completely new life. Prior to her illness we had always been inseparable. I just loved to be with her and hold her hand wherever we went. People commented on it. If ever I needed to be away, even if only for a night, I felt bereft and talked to her endlessly on the phone. Sometimes Sue would laugh and tell me that I talked to her more when I was away than when we were together. Perhaps that was true, for one of the most beautiful things about a very special friendship is that the silences aren't awkward and that just being together is a delight.

As a result, simply getting used to being without her has been a steep learning curve. It's not just having to clean (at least occasionally) or to cook for myself (though what I do doesn't deserve the description 'cooking'). It is simply learning to carry on without Sue that has been so very hard.

Some things about it have shocked me. I expected to feel very tired after the funeral. I knew that I had been under great strain as I sought to meet her needs and be strong for her in the last months of her life. I knew, too, that adrenaline had carried me through the busy days up to the funeral and a little beyond. Yet the utter weariness that assailed me in the weeks that followed was a real surprise.

So was the related dip in my general health. I spent two separate nights in hospital within six weeks of Sue's death. The provisional diagnosis was angina, but the problem proved to be nothing to do with my heart, whatever the symptoms appeared to say. The real issue was the effects that stress had put on my gastric system. In response I have learned the value of eating less and more healthily, including lots of lovely green vegetables. I have also put regular walks of a mile or two every day into my schedule, with pleasing results.

Furthermore, I have understood, with my mind at least, the need to get plenty of sleep. Thankfully, all my life I have slept well, and still do, though sometimes when I wake to visit the bathroom I'm shocked by how little time has elapsed since I came to bed. However, I have a real problem with actually *getting* to bed.

Sue and I always went to bed together and, although *she* was the night bird, in recent years she often had to nag *me* to turn in. Now that she isn't there, I am more inclined to faff around than ever, and often revert to watching the 24-

hour news or sending yet another email when I should be getting to bed. Indeed it is usually after midnight before I turn in. The explanation is simple. There's no real incentive to be there: no one to chat to, or cuddle for that matter. I don't dread the lonely bedroom: it's just not the inviting place — the social space — it once was. Yet I do realise that having less sleep means asking for trouble.

One thing I did quickly learn, and have often found myself needing to explain to others, is that there is all the difference in the world between missing someone and being lonely. I miss Sue tremendously. I find it really hard to be without her. She was such a fun person and almost always great company. She could talk interestingly and intelligently about a vast range of subjects. She was by far my closest, best and most valued friend. I feel bereft without her. But I am not lonely: not at all. And why is that?

Well, there are lots of reasons. I am blessed with a caring family whose company I treasure. It is a beautiful thing to have a deep friendship with grown-up children — friendship on an equal footing — and doubly so since all my offspring love and follow my Saviour. Also I have a huge number of kind and thoughtful friends who seem not only to care deeply about how I am doing, but to value my company. On top of that I quite enjoy times when I am on my own: being alone fairly frequently doesn't bother me. So I'm not lonely: but it is a great hardship to be without my Sue.

Being one flesh with her was so much more than sexual

union, however beautiful and affirming that was for us both. She really was my 'other half'. That means that half of me is now missing. And no-one can make up for that loss, not even the Lord Himself! Don't misunderstand me. We all have a profound, supreme need for fellowship with God, whether we recognise it or not. Yet, it was God Himself who said of sinless Adam, 'It is not good for man to be alone'. And Adam had the privilege of walking with God in a perfect, curse-free world. The simple fact is that God has made us social beings, and built into our DNA is the need for human companionship.

Clearly marriage is not the only solution to man's social need. All close human friendship is a glorious, eminently satisfying and supportive blessing. Not being married doesn't have to mean an empty and miserable life. Yet having been married, and having grown incredibly close to a special companion, often means that when that person dies a hole is left that it is impossible to fill.

I am glad to say that some things about my new life have not proved as difficult as I feared. So far I've not found those special days — our wedding anniversary, Valentine's Day, Sue's birthday (or even the day she died), Christmas Day, and the like — any more difficult than the next day. Indeed, I have found that the 'special days' often prompt a flood of very special memories that cause great joy. It's a temperamental thing: at least one of my girls finds such days (including Mothers' Day) a great trial. So I pray for others and thank the Lord that he's made me different from many.

Thankfully, too, I have stumbled upon lots of practical helps that make the painful business of living without Sue somewhat easier. Unlike some men, I find an almost inexpressible joy in poring over photographs of Sue. They never fail to make me smile and lift my spirits. I find it particularly delightful when I discover, or am given, new snaps to add to my collection. One obvious reason for that joyful reaction is that pretty well every picture prompts lovely memories of incidents or stages in our life together, and sets my heart to singing.

It is equally helpful when others talk to me about her, and remind me of incidents that show off some of her many qualities. It is also reassuring when people listen to me appreciatively when I prattle on about her. And it is especially valuable when others in a similar situation openly talk about their own experience of losing a wife, and things that have helped them to cope.

One dear man, in the church pastored by my son Phil in Yate, has been particularly helpful. Firstly, shortly after I lost Sue, he sent me a small but very helpful book for Christians about coping with bereavement. It's by Al Martin and is called 'Grieving, Hope and Solace'. I heartily recommend it, particularly to widowers. Better still, he has since allowed me to quiz him about his own experience of losing his wife, and especially how he has benefitted from moving into a 'grandad flat' in his daughter's family home. I am sure that David has little idea of the blessing and encouragement his willingness to share his own experience has been to me.

I have found that keeping busy has also been a considerable help in my efforts to resist all temptation towards wallowing in self-pity. Sadly, little of that busyness has been domestic, with the result that our home, which was legendary roundabouts for its cleanness and especially its tidiness — even when five children lived here — is both dusty and very messy. Also within eighteen months of her death both gardens had reverted to wilderness conditions, though thankfully the front one has been rescued through the heroic efforts of our Jo and her husband Michael.

In truth, I prefer almost anything to domestic duties, so most of my spare time is filled with visiting or phoning friends and family, reading, walking and the odd visit to a National Trust property or the Keighley and Worth Valley Railway, where being a life-member means free travel. I've also taken occasionally to watching professional football again for the first time in decades — usually suffering with the loyal supporters of AFC Guiseley. But it all helps to keep me on an even keel, mentally and emotionally.

For me, keeping busy has largely meant returning to almost full-time work and so living the life that Sue told me, while she was still well, was her 'nightmare scenario' for my retirement — 'same job, same hours, no pay'! Yet, without her to share my life, that path has proved very helpful to me.

As well as continuing to do some pastoral visitation for DEC, I've become very involved with our attempt to plant a new church in the city of Wakefield. The team of around twenty are almost all at least young enough to be my children and treat this pensioner with affection, respect and great kindness. It is a venture that Sue and I had long desired and prayed for, and it is very satisfying to be able to play a small part in encouraging those involved in the hard graft of the work. Indeed, it has been a really significant way in which the Lord has kept my spirits up as I have grieved over my loss.

On top of that I have become involved in a pastoral support ministry for the workers of SASRA, an organisation committed to offering spiritual help and human friendship to personnel in our armed forces. Their executive director, Andrew Hill, has been a friend for decades, and after Sue's death he approached me requesting my help in supporting their staff, especially those who seek to maintain a winsome testimony on army camps and RAF bases across the UK. So far that contact and ministry have brought me nothing but joy.

I cannot pretend, however, that anything can adequately compensate for having lost my lovely wife. Even though life without her still has its delights, and provides so many reasons for gratitude to my heavenly Father, yet it has become increasingly apparent to me that her promotion to glory in the presence of the Saviour she served so faithfully by my side has left a huge hole in my life. The truth is, you don't get married to live on your own, so to come to that after so long, and such happiness, is relentlessly distressing.

However, I have been both surprised and heartened to find that, so far at least, I have not been troubled by a bitter spirit over having lost Sue, and especially at a time when we were greatly looking forward to the future. Indeed, even moments of wretched self-pity have, mercifully, been few and far between.

It is not easy to analyse why that is, although I believe it to be God's grace at work in answer to the prayers of many. The simplest explanation of it in terms of my thought process is this. Whenever I think of Sue, and my life with her for around forty-five years, I feel overwhelmingly thankful. Therefore, it just seems so unnatural to start complaining and being angry about the fact that she has at last been taken from me. She wasn't perfect, certainly not. Yet she was a wonderful wife and a wonderful gift that I have done nothing to deserve. To be bitter and twisted about having lost her just seems to me like arrogance and ingratitude of monstrous proportions. I pray that it may ever do so!

FIFTEEN

Consolations rich and real

My most effective weapons against despair

THOUGH IT IS NOW MORE than two years since I lost Sue, friends still sometimes take my hand, look me in the eye with an anxious expression, and ask me how I am doing. It is a question born of loving concern, but I never find it an easy one to answer. I believe there are two key reasons for that.

Firstly, my mood can change very quickly. Gloom can strike suddenly and unexpectedly after days, or even weeks, of feeling pretty cheerful. Secondly, I have never been good at reading my own heart. I am neither a deep thinker, nor particularly introspective. As a result I often find it hard to tell how I'm really doing. In truth, I often just muddle along with life without giving much thought as to whether I'm coping or not.

What I do know, however, is that I am constantly kept

from despair, and crippling grief over my loss, by two key tenets of my Christian faith. The first is the confidence that, like all who die with trust in Jesus the Saviour, Sue has not ceased to exist but is more alive than ever, living in heaven. Indeed, my Bible has further taught me that she is awaiting the day of Christ's return when her precious body will be reanimated, transformed, and reunited with her spirit. My second greatly reassuring conviction is that my God and Father will help and bless me all my days here so that I'm never reduced to an empty or meaningless 'half-life.'

Confidence concerning Sue

The first of those convictions often brings a reaction of scorn or pity. How can a seemingly intelligent man possibly believe that his dead wife lives on, and even that her rapidly decaying body will one day be raised to life? Isn't that just the foolish refusal of a weak, distressed mind to face the stubborn realities of death, human decay and the evident finality of the grave? I do not believe that it is, and that for what I am confident are good reasons.

The careful historian Luke, writing to his friend Theophilus in a document you can find in the second half of the Bible, tells us of a day towards the end of Jesus' life on earth when he went up a mountain to pray, taking his friends Peter, James and John with him. You can read his detailed account of what happened to them there in the ninth chapter of his Gospel. Basically, while they were with him they witnessed strange things that were so burnt into their minds that Peter could write about them thirty years later as if they had happened yesterday (see his second letter chapter 1, towards the end of the Bible).

On that mountain Jesus' appearance changed. He began to radiate a strange, other-worldly glory. Even his clothes shone brightly. Then, seemingly out of nowhere, Moses and Elijah, two of the most famous figures in Jewish history, appeared bodily — solid and very real — talking to Jesus. Moses had been dead for fifteen hundred years! Elijah hadn't been seen in this world for around half that time. Yet here they were, talking with Jesus about the death he would shortly die in Jerusalem, and talking about it as a triumphant achievement of long-laid plans. Here is irrefutable proof that at least some of the dead live on.

But did it really happen? Isn't it much more likely that the story is a fable — a pack of lies? No, it isn't. If you take time to look at it carefully, Luke's account has a number of striking indications that he is writing a simple account of things that really took place. Though it is a dramatic story, it is written in a very sober, matter-of-fact way. Furthermore, it contains details that you would never include if you were trying to foist fables onto a sceptical public.

Luke admits, for example, that Jesus' friends were just beginning to doze when the heroes of old appeared. He also reports that Peter, the most celebrated of the disciples, could only mouth inconsequential foolishness in response to what he saw, and that those 'stars' of the early church were frightened when the cloud started to envelop them.

Those are telling indications that Luke is writing sober history.

The riposte of many is simply and airily to deny that such things could happen. And even those who are more interested in seeking truth than simply preserving their scepticism usually say there is something in Luke's report that demonstrates that he *cannot* be telling the truth. He claims that 'the disciples kept this (extraordinary experience) to themselves and did not tell anyone what they had seen'!

Surely that is psychologically impossible. Could you have done that? Could I? Yes, if we had, like them, just heard the very voice of God himself tell us to listen to Jesus, and the one thing he pressed upon us was not to tell others what we had witnessed until he had risen from the dead (see Matthew's account of the same incident, Matthew 17:9)! Such an experience would have brought a great, mind-controlling fear of disobeying the mighty God.

Perhaps we need two further pieces of the jigsaw in order to be confronted by the sober truth of Luke's strange account. The first is to see that this story fits with Luke's whole, well researched and plainly written story of Jesus' life which is stubbornly supernatural from beginning to end. The second is to grasp the Bible's wider explanation of this incident that is generally called the 'Transfiguration'.

Luke shows us that Moses and Elijah came from heaven to encourage Jesus as he faced the horror of what lay ahead of him. His Father spoke audibly to the same effect, declaring that he was 'well pleased' with his Son. And the human occupants of heaven who met with him were preoccupied with that coming death because it was to be unique, *and* vital to them.

Paul, the spokesman of Jesus Christ, explains why that is in Romans chapter three. He affirms that by his death Jesus paid the penalty for human sin (3:24-25). That achieved two vital things. Firstly, it vindicates God's justice in pardoning and admitting to heaven sinful people, like Moses and Elijah, who humbly look to him for mercy on the basis of all the Saviour has done (3:25).

In addition, it means not only that God's promises of mercy to humbled sinners would fail if he abandoned them to the grave, but that his justice would be violated as well! Since Christ has paid in full for all his people's failings, not only must he be vindicated by bodily resurrection — as indeed he was — but none of his people must be allowed to remain for ever in the grave, under the power of death which is the 'wages of sin' (Romans 6:23).

Hence my confidence regarding Sue, a flawed woman who trusted not in the quality of her life but only in Jesus and his atoning death for her acceptance with God. It is because of what God has done in Christ that I believe that she is in the glorious presence of Christ right now. And the same reliance on all God has said and done assures me also that her body will one day be raised in power to be reunited, gloriously transformed, to her precious soul. Although seeing and glorying in Christ is my great hope for the future, the thought of meeting Sue again is an exciting, delightful and reassuring prospect also, and plays a big part in keeping my grief from becoming overwhelming.

The assurance of God's shepherdly care

My second great comfort in my loss is the many promises that God has made in his word to humbled sinners like me. Those promises are beautifully illustrated in the Shepherd Psalm, Psalm 23, penned by David, Israel's shepherd-king. That psalm became far more personal to me during the events of the story I've retold in this little book, and its words have continued to thrill and sustain me ever since.

One of the psalm's great values is to teach us what religion at its best is all about. It's not, as many imagine, about believing the unbelievable, or about strange religious rituals. Nor is it primarily about all the things God insists that you mustn't do in life. Sure there are truths we must believe, and rituals to perform that provide great reassurance to faith. And there are wise instructions for life, some of which are expressed negatively, However, the Shepherd Psalm shouts loudly that real religion is supremely about a relationship with the only real God, and all the glorious things that flow to the person who enjoys that relationship. This is clear from the very first verse, where David humbly declares, 'The LORD is my Shepherd', and from that draws the fully warranted and wonderfully reassuring conclusion, 'I will lack nothing'.

The picture David gives us is of a real and intimate relationship of leadership and dependence. In Old

Testament times Jewish shepherds lived with their sheep. They led them to pastures to eat and rest in, and to streams to drink from even in seasons of drought. They were the vets and guardians of the sheep, totally responsible for their welfare. And while the image is a humbling one - for sheep are foolish, awkward, stubborn, fearful and vulnerable - for the Christian it is a very reassuring picture of our Lord.

The whole psalm breathes the confidence that flows from knowing that the Lord is *my* God. That confidence doesn't come from some foolish notion about life being easy from the day of making peace with God. David tells us there will be dark valleys and enemies, as well as our tendency to wander. Yet it shouts to me, as one he has drawn to trust in His dear Son as my Saviour and Lord, that I too can have confidence that he will be my Shepherd.

And what exactly does that mean, in practical terms? The psalm tells me so clearly. It means that my covenant God will always be at work in my life for my wellbeing, day after day (verses 2-3). Better still, it means that he will more than look after me in life's harshest experiences, like facing death or bereavement, loneliness or opposition (verses 4-5). Finally, it means that I need not fear the future, a reassurance I desperately need. The Spirit of God assures me through David that my great Shepherd will be good and loving to me all the days of my life here, and then will welcome me to an unimaginably glorious future in his presence in the world to come (verse 6).

It is these two convictions — the reality of heaven for

pardoned sinners and the assurance of God's care as my Shepherd — that have, above all other things, quietened my heart, lifted my spirits, and given me hope in the face of losing the lady whose presence so enriched my life for over forty-five years. Here I have found reasons to sing again, and shelter from the biting winds of grief, loneliness and fear.

Indeed, I have written this account of my journey, through my precious Sue's dreadful experience and beyond, to testify that the Lord - the awesome, majestic and unfathomable God - has indeed walked with this poor, sinful, frightened and stubborn sinner through the dreadful valley of the shadow of death. And I want to affirm that all this time he has relentlessly pursued me with his goodness and his covenant love and faithfulness, just as David knew he always would (see verse 6). To that I cling as I press on in the still blessed, though less colourful, life that I walk without the dear woman whose ring I continue to wear.

Postscript

A joyful new beginning: yet more of heaven's kindness

After completing the basic manuscript of this little book my life took a surprising and delightful turn in April 2018, when I began a sweet relationship with a new lady friend. Barbara Brown had arrived at Dewsbury Evangelical Church the previous autumn, having moved into the town from Manchester, where she had lived for forty years, about half of them as a widow. However, all that time she had retained an accent that pleasingly reveals her Belfast origins.

Barbara had come across the Pennines to help her daughter Anna, living in South Leeds, cope with two sets of young twins. She quickly settled into the church and soon established a reputation there for a cheerful disposition and a readiness to serve in whatever way she could.

Over time I found myself noticing her more and more,

and coming to appreciate evident faith, her kindness, her gentle words and her fun-loving spirit. So I began to wrestle with the idea of asking her out. I distinctly remember feeling very self-conscious, lacking confidence and fearing the pain and embarrassment of rejection. It was as if I was a teenager all over again!

However, one evening at a social event I found myself emboldened to sit next to her, and found it easy and natural to suggest that she might like to join me on a visit to the National Trust's beautiful Dunham Massey — not far from her former home in Chorlton-cum-Hardy — to meet our only truly long-term mutual friends, Steve and Ishbel Saxton. I was relieved and very pleased to get an instantly positive response.

From that small beginning the friendship grew speedily, some might say like wildfire, stimulated by brief walks and longer conversations — including by phone when I was away. Engagement followed quickly, and then plans for marriage.

With the love and good wishes of our families and many kind friends, we were married at Dewsbury Evangelical Church on Saturday December 1st, 2018. Thus started, in the kindness of our God and Father, a new delightful and unexpected chapter of life for us both, proving the truth of some words with which I had closed an article written some eighteen months earlier for Evangelical Times, under the title, 'Home Alone: A Christian Widower's struggle'.

There I had written these almost prophetic words:

Who knows what joys and blessings the Lord still has in store for me. So I need to grasp again that every day with him is an adventure into the unknown, in which his grace will always prove sufficient and his mercies new and surprising.